Dietrich Bonhoeffer

LETTERS AND PAPERS
FROM PRISON

edited by Eberhard Bethge

An Abridged Edition

SCM PRESS LTD

The text of this abridgment
has been newly revised throughout by John Bowden.
It was made from The Enlarged Edition 1971
which was translated from the German
Widerstand und Ergebung
Briefe und Aufzeichnungen aus der Haft
(Chr. Kaiser Verlag, new ed., Munich 1970)
and incorporates the text of the third English edition
produced by Reginald Fuller, Frank Clarke and others,
with additional material translated by John Bowden

334 00895 6

First published in English 1953
by SCM Press Ltd
26–30 Tottenham Road London N1
Second (enlarged) edition 1956
Third edition, revised and enlarged, 1967
Fourth edition (The Enlarged Edition) 1971
This Abridged Edition 1981
Second impression 1985

Photoset by John Smith, London
and printed in Great Britain by
Richard Clay (The Chaucer Press) Ltd
Bungay, Suffolk

Contents

Publisher's Note

If you are coming to this classic of twentieth-century religion for the first time, you will need a little background information. But not much; these remarkable writings virtually speak for themselves.

On 5 April 1943, Dietrich Bonhoeffer, an exceptionally gifted theologian and pastor, who had also been director of a seminary in the anti-Hitler Confessing Church, was arrested on suspicion of comparatively minor offences. Through his family, however, he had been actively involved with the *Abwehr*, the German security organization, which contained a focal point for opposition to Hitler and was even connected with attempts on his life. Bonhoeffer was taken to Tegel prison, in Berlin, where he spent the next eighteen months while investigations were made; on 8 October 1944 he was transferred to the Gestapo prison in Prinz Albrecht Strasse, after the discovery of documents proving his involvement, along with that of other senior figures, in conspiracy. Evacuated from Berlin after heavy bombing of this prison, he was finally hanged in Flossenbürg prison camp on 9 April 1945. One of his brothers and the husbands of two sisters were also executed.

Of the letters included here, all but the last, to his mother, were written from Tegel prison. Those to his parents had to pass through the prison censorship, and were also seen by the man investigating his case, so here certain things, quite obvious to those to whom the letters are addressed, were written for the censors; the other letters, to Bonhoeffer's closest friend Eberhard Bethge, were smuggled out by friendly guards at the prison. The correspondence continued after the last letter included here, but had to be destroyed for security reasons, not least because Bethge himself was later arrested. During the time Bonhoeffer was in prison, Eberhard Bethge married his niece Renate Schleicher, so the papers written in Tegel include a wedding sermon for them, and 'thoughts' on the baptism of their son Dietrich, named after Bonhoeffer. There are also many references to Maria von

Wedemeyer, Bonhoeffer's young fiancée, to whom he had become engaged only shortly before his arrest.

No explanatory notes have been included in this edition; those wanting more detailed information will find it either in the full edition of *Letters and Papers from Prison* or in the other books mentioned for further reading.

Those already familiar with *Letters and Papers* will want to know how this new version differs from its predecessors. *Letters and Papers* was first published in English by SCM Press in 1953 in a translation by Reginald Fuller, a revised edition of which became the basis for the immensely popular Fontana Books edition of 1959. Although this translation was attractive to read, close study, particularly of the revolutionary theological thoughts towards the end, showed that it was so free that it sometimes quite seriously misrepresented Bonhoeffer. Consequently, a substantially revised translation was published by SCM Press in 1967. To complicate the story further, in 1970, to commemorate the twenty-fifth anniversary of Bonhoeffer's death, the Bethges released a great deal more material, including many letters to Bonhoeffer as well as from him, and documents concerned with his case, which were published as *Letters and Papers from Prison. The Enlarged Edition*, by SCM Press in 1971. This edition also contains an article by Bonhoeffer's fiancée, quoting from letters which he wrote to her.

Valuable though it is to have the wealth of material now included in the enlarged edition of *Letters and Papers*, three times the size of the present volume, and essential though that edition will always be, there is no doubt that the extra documentation slows down the story, complicates its forward movement, and dulls the impact made by the original version. It seems that there is also room for a text to introduce Bonhoeffer to a new generation, in which his experiences and his intellectual exploration stand out starkly and clearly. There is less material here than in any previous edition, but we hope that nothing important has been omitted; what we have done can be seen by anyone checking with the enlarged edition. In content it comes closest to the first edition, but in passages included the fuller personal references of the later editions have been kept.

The Bethges have been kindness itself in looking over the abridgment. At their prompting the whole translation has been checked through yet again and further inadequacies have been corrected; they would want us in particular to draw attention to the occurrence of 'now' in connection with Isa. 53 in the letter of 18 July 1944, and the revisions of 'Outline for a Book' and 'Stations on the Road to Freedom'. However, the idea for the abridgment was ours, not theirs, and any criticisms of the way in which it has been carried out must be directed to us.

For Further Reading

Eberhard Bethge, *Dietrich Bonhoeffer: Theologian, Christian, Contemporary*, Collins 1970; Fount Books 1977
  The definitive, full-length biography of Dietrich Bonhoeffer

Eberhard Bethge, *Bonhoeffer: An Illustrated Introduction*, Fount Books 1979
  A much shorter text, with a great many contemporary illustrations

Mary Bosanquet, *Bonhoeffer. True Patriot*, Mowbray 1978
  Perhaps the most attractive biography for English readers, first published by Hodder and Stoughton under the title *The Life and Death of Dietrich Bonhoeffer*, in 1968

Dietrich Bonhoeffer, *Life Together*, SCM Press 1954
  Communal Christian life according to Bonhoeffer's ideals, dating from his time as director of the Finkenwalde seminary

Dietrich Bonhoeffer, *Ethics*, SCM Press 1955
  His last, unfinished book, written just before his arrest

Dietrich Bonhoeffer, *Letters and Papers from Prison. The Enlarged Edition*, SCM Press 1971

To his parents 14 April 1943

I do want you to be quite sure that I'm all right. I'm sorry that I was not allowed to write to you sooner, but I was all right during the first ten days too. Strangely enough, the discomforts that one generally associates with prison life, the physical hardships, hardly bother me at all. One can even have enough to eat in the mornings with dry bread (I get a variety of extras too). The hard prison bed does not worry me a bit, and one can get plenty of sleep between 8 p.m. and 6 a.m. I have been particularly surprised that I have hardly felt any need at all for cigarettes since I came here; but I think that in all this psychological factors have played a decisive role. A violent mental upheaval such as is produced by a sudden arrest brings with it the need to take one's mental bearings and come to terms with an entirely new situation – all this means that physical things take a back seat and lose their importance, and it is something that I find to be a real enrichment of my experience. I am not so unused to being alone as other people are, and it is certainly a good spiritual Turkish bath. The only thing that bothers me or would bother me is the thought that you are being tormented by anxiety about me, and are not sleeping or eating properly. Forgive me for causing you so much worry, but I think a hostile fate is more to blame than I am. To set off against that, it is good to read Paul Gerhardt's hymns and learn them by heart, as I am doing now. Besides that, I have my Bible and some reading matter from the library here, and enough writing paper now.

You can imagine that I'm most particularly anxious about my fiancée at the moment. It's a great deal for her to bear, especially when she has only recently lost her father and brother in the East. As the daughter of an officer, she will perhaps find my imprisonment especially hard to take. If only I could have a few words with her! Now you will have to do it. Perhaps she will come to you in Berlin. That would be fine.

1

The seventy-fifth birthday celebrations were a fortnight ago today. It was a splendid day. I can still hear the chorale that we sang in the morning and evening, with all the voices and instruments: 'Praise to the Lord, the Almighty, the King of Creation... Shelters thee under his wings, yea, and gently sustaineth.' That is true, and it is what we must always rely on.

Spring is really coming now. You will have plenty to do in the garden; I hope that Renate's wedding preparations are going well. Here in the prison yard there is a thrush which sings beautifully in the morning, and now in the evening too. One is grateful for little things, and that is surely a gain. Good-bye for now.

I'm thinking of you and the rest of the family and my friends with gratitude and love,   your Dietrich

When you have the chance, could you leave here for me slippers, bootlaces (black, long), shoe polish, writing paper and envelopes, ink, smoker's card, shaving cream, sewing things and a suit I can change into? Many thanks for everything.

To his parents   Easter Day, 25 April 1943

At last the tenth day has come round, and I'm allowed to write to you again; I'm so glad to let you know that even here I'm having a happy Easter. Good Friday and Easter free us to think about other things far beyond our own personal fate, about the ultimate meaning of all life, suffering, and events; and we lay hold of a great hope. Since yesterday it has been marvellously quiet in the house. I heard many people wishing each other a happy Easter, and one does not begrudge it anyone who is on duty here – it's a hard job. In the stillness now I can also hear your Easter greetings, if you're together with the family today and thinking of me...

Things are still all right, and I am well. I'm allowed out of doors for half an hour every day, and now that I can smoke again, I even forget sometimes, for a little while, where I am! I'm being treated well, and I read a good deal – newspapers, novels, and above all the Bible. I can't concentrate enough yet for serious work, but during Holy Week I at last managed to work solidly through a part of the passion story that has occupied me a great deal for a long time – the high-priestly prayer. I've even been able to expound to

2

myself a few chapters of Pauline ethical material; I felt that to be very important. So I really have a great deal to be very thankful for...

It is surprising how quickly the days pass here. I can hardly believe that I have been here three weeks. I like going to bed at eight o'clock (supper is at four!), and I look forward to my dreams. I never knew before what a source of pleasure that can be; I dream every day, and always about something pleasant. Before I go to sleep I repeat to myself the verses that I have learnt during the day, and at 6 a.m. I like to read psalms and hymns, think of you all, and know that you are thinking of me...

To his parents   5 May 1943

... I've now had four weeks in prison; and whereas I was able from the outset to accept my lot consciously, I'm now getting used to it in a kind of natural and unconscious way. That is a relief, but it raises problems of its own, for one rightly does not want to get used to being in this position; I think you will feel the same way about it.

You want to know more about my life here. To picture a cell does not need much imagination – the less you use, the nearer the mark you will be. At Easter the *Deutsche Allgemeine Zeitung* brought out a reproduction from Dürer's *Apocalypse*, which I pinned up on the wall; and some of Maria's primulas are still here too. Our day lasts fourteen hours, of which I spend about three walking up and down the cell – several kilometres a day, besides half an hour in the yard. I read, learn, and work. I particularly enjoyed reading Gotthelf again, with his clear, wholesome, serene style. I'm getting on all right and keeping well...

I often think here of that lovely song of Hugo Wolf's, which we have sung several times lately:

> In the night, in the night, come joy and woe,
> Before you're aware, away they go,
> To God their message bearing
> Of how they've found you faring.

It all turns on that 'how', which is more important than anything that happens to you from outside. It allays all the anxieties about the future which sometimes torment us...

3

... People outside find it difficult to imagine what prison life is like. The situation in itself – that is each single moment – is perhaps not so very different here from anywhere else; I read, meditate, write, pace up and down my cell – without rubbing myself sore against the walls like a polar bear. The great thing is to stick to what one still has and can do – there is still plenty left – and not to be dominated by the thought of what one cannot do, and by feelings of resentment and discontent. I'm sure I never realized as clearly as I do here what the Bible and Luther mean by 'temptation'. Quite suddenly, and for no apparent physical or psychological reason, the peace and composure that were supporting one are jarred, and the heart becomes, in Jeremiah's expressive phrase, 'deceitful above all things, and desperately corrupt; who can understand it?' It feels like an invasion from outside, as if by evil powers trying to rob one of what is most vital. But no doubt these experiences are good and necessary, as they teach one to understand human life better.

I'm now trying my hand at a little study on 'The feeling of time', an experience specially relevant to anyone who is being held for examination. One of my predecessors here has scribbled over the cell door, 'In 100 years it will be over.' That was his way of trying to counter the feeling that life spent here is a blank; but there is a great deal that might be said about that, and I should like to talk it over with father. 'My time is in your hands' (Ps. 31) is the Bible's answer. But in the Bible there is also the question that threatens to dominate everything here: 'How long, O Lord?' (Ps. 13)...

Many thanks for the Jeremias Gotthelf. In a fortnight I would very much like his *Uli der Knecht*. Renate has it. By the way, you really ought to read his *Berner Geist*, and if not the whole of it, at least the first part; it is something out of the ordinary, and it will certainly interest you. I remember how old Schöne always had a special word of praise for Gotthelf, and I should like to suggest to the Diederich Press that they bring out a Gotthelf day-book. Stifter's background, too, is mainly Christian; his woodland scenes often make me long to be back again in the quiet glades of Friedrichsbrunn. He is not so forceful as Gotthelf, but he is wonderfully clear and simple, and that gives me a great deal of pleasure. If only we could talk to each other about these things! For all my sympathy with the contemplative life, I am not a born Trappist. Nevertheless, a period of enforced silence may be a good thing, and the Roman Catholics say that the most effective expositions of scripture come from the purely contemplative orders. I am reading the Bible straight through from cover to cover, and have just got as far as Job, which I am particularly fond of. I read the Psalms every day, as I have done for years; I know them and love them more than any other book. I cannot now read Psalms 3, 47, 70, and others without hearing them in the settings by Heinrich Schütz. It was Renate who introduced me to his music, and I count it one of the greatest enrichments of my life. . .

A Wedding Sermon from a Prison Cell
May 1943

Eph. 1.12: 'We who . . . have been destined and appointed
to live for the praise of his glory.'

It is right and proper for a bride and bridegroom to welcome and celebrate their wedding day with a unique sense of triumph. When all the difficulties, obstacles, hindrances, doubts, and misgivings have been, not made light of, but honestly faced and overcome – and it is certainly better not to take everything for granted – then both parties have indeed achieved the most important triumph of their lives. With the 'Yes' that they have said to each other, they have by their free choice given a new direction to their lives; they have cheerfully and confidently defied all the uncertainties and hesitations with which, as they know, a lifelong partnership between two people is faced; and by their own free and responsible action they have conquered a new land to live in. Every wedding must be an occasion of joy that human beings can do such great things, that they have been given such immense freedom and power to take the helm in their life's journey. The children of the earth are rightly proud of being allowed to take a hand in shaping their own destinies, and something of this pride must contribute to the happiness of a bride and bridegroom. We ought not to be in too much of a hurry here to speak piously of God's will and guidance. It is obvious, and it should not be ignored, that it is your own very human wills that are at work here, celebrating their triumph; the course that you are taking at the outset is one that you have chosen for yourselves; what you have done and are doing is not, in the first place, something religious, but something quite worldly. So you yourselves, and you alone, bear the responsibility for what no one can take from you; or, to put it more exactly, you, Eberhard, have all the responsibility for the success of your venture, with all the happiness that such responsibility involves, and you, Renate, will help your husband and make it easy for him to bear that responsibility, and find your happiness in that. Unless you can boldly say today: 'That is *our* resolve, *our* love, *our* way', you are taking refuge in a false piety. 'Iron and steel may pass away, but *our* love shall abide for ever.' That desire for earthly bliss, which you want to find in one another, and in which, to quote the medieval song, one is the comfort of the other both in body and in soul – that desire is justified before God and man.

Certainly you two, of all people, have every reason to look back with special thankfulness on your lives up to now. The beautiful things and the joys of life have been showered on you, you have succeeded in everything, and you have been surrounded by love and friendship. Your ways have, for the most part, been smoothed before you took them, and you have always been able to count on the support of your families and friends. Everyone has wished you well, and now it has been given to you to find each other and to reach the goal of your desires. You yourselves know that no one can create and assume such a life from his own strength, but that what is given to one is withheld from another; and however confidently you accept responsibility for your action today, you may and will put it today with equal confidence into God's hands.

As God today adds his 'Yes' to your 'Yes', as he confirms your will with his will, and as he allows you, and approves of, your triumph and rejoicing and pride, he makes you at the same time instruments of his will and purpose both for yourselves and for others. In his unfathomable condescension God does add his 'Yes' to yours; but by doing so, he creates out of your love something quite new – the holy estate of matrimony.

God is guiding your marriage. Marriage is more than your love for each other. It has a higher dignity and power, for it is God's holy ordinance, through which he wills to perpetuate the human race till the end of time. In your love you see only your two selves in the world, but in marriage you are a link in the chain of the generations, which God causes to come and to pass away to his glory, and calls into his kingdom. In your love you see only the heaven of your own happiness, but in marriage you are placed at a post of responsibility towards the world and mankind. Your love is your own private possession, but marriage is more than something personal – it is a status, an office. Just as it is the crown, and not merely the will to rule, that makes the king, so it is marriage, and not merely your love for each other, that joins you together in the sight of God and man. As you first gave the ring to one another and have now received it a second time from the hand of the pastor, so love comes from you, but marriage from above, from God. As high as God is above man, so high are the sanctity, the rights, and the promise of marriage above the sanctity, the rights, and the promise of love. It is not your love that sustains the marriage, but from now on, the marriage that sustains your love.

God makes your marriage indissoluble. 'What therefore God has joined together, let no man put asunder' (Matt. 19.6). God joins you together in marriage; it is his act, not yours. Do not confound your love for one another with God. God makes your marriage indissoluble, and protects it from every danger that may threaten it from within and without; he wills to be the guarantor of its indissolubility. It is a blessed thing to know that no power on earth, no temptation, no human frailty can dissolve what God holds together; indeed, anyone who knows that may say confidently: What God has joined together, *can* no man put asunder. Free from all the anxiety that is always a characteristic of love, you can now say to each other with complete and confident assurance: We can never lose each other now; by the will of God we belong to each other till death.

God establishes an order in which you can live together in wedlock. 'Wives, be subject to your husbands, as is fitting in the Lord. Husbands, love your wives' (Col. 3). With your marriage you are founding a home. That needs an order, and this order is so important that God establishes it himself, because without it everything would get out of joint. You may order your home as you like, except in one thing: the wife is to be subject to her husband, and the husband is to love his wife. In this way God gives to husband and wife the honour that is due to each. The wife's honour is to serve the husband, to be a 'help meet for him', as the creation story has it; and the husband's honour is to love his wife with all his heart. He will 'leave his father and mother and be joined to his wife', and will 'love her as his own flesh'. A wife who wants to dominate her husband dishonours herself and him, just as a husband who does not love his wife as he should dishonours himself and her; and both dishonour the glory of God that is meant to rest on the estate of matrimony. It is an unhealthy state of affairs when the wife's ambition is to be like the husband, and the husband regards the wife merely as the plaything of his own lust for power and licence; and it is a sign of social disintegration when the wife's service is felt to be degrading or beneath her dignity, and when the husband who is faithful to his wife is looked on as a weakling or even a fool.

The place where God has put the wife is the husband's home. Most people have forgotten nowadays what a home can mean, though some of us have come to realize it as never before. It is a kingdom of its own in the midst of the world, a stronghold amid life's storms and stresses, a refuge, even a sanctuary. It is not founded on the shifting sands of outward or public life, but it has its resting place in God, for God gives it its special meaning and value, its own nature and privilege, its own destiny and dignity. It is an ordinance of God in the world, the place in which – whatever may happen in the world – peace, quietness, joy, love, purity, discipline, respect, obedience, tradition, and, with it all, happiness may dwell. It is the wife's calling, and her happiness, to build up for her husband this world within the world, and to do her life's work there. How happy she is if she realizes how great and rich a task and destiny she has. Not novelty, but permanence; not change, but constancy; not noisiness, but peace; not words, but deeds; not commands, but persuasion; not desire, but possession – and all these things inspired and sustained by her love for her husband –, that is the wife's kingdom. In the Book of Proverbs we read: 'The heart of her husband trusts in her, and he will have no lack of gain. She does him good, and not harm, all the days of her life. She seeks wool and flax, and works with willing hands... She

8

rises while it is yet night and provides food for her household and tasks for her maidens... She opens her hand to the poor, and reaches out her hands to the needy ... Strength and dignity are her clothing, and she laughs at the time to come ... Her children rise up and call her blessed; her husband also, and he praises her ... Many women have done excellently, but you surpass them all.' Again and again the Bible praises, as the supreme earthly happiness, the fortune of a man who finds a true, or as the Bible puts it, a 'virtuous' or 'wise' woman. 'She is far more precious than jewels.' 'A virtuous woman is the crown of her husband.' But the Bible speaks just as frankly of the mischief that a perverse, 'foolish' woman brings on her husband and her home.

Now when the husband is called 'the head of the wife', and it goes on to say 'as Christ is the head of the church', something of the divine splendour is reflected in our earthly relationships, and this reflection we should recognize and honour. The dignity that is here ascribed to the man lies, not in any capacities or qualities of his own, but in the office conferred on him by his marriage. The wife should see her husband clothed in this dignity. But for him it is a supreme responsibility. As the head, it is he who is responsible for his wife, for their marriage, and for their home. On him falls the care and protection of the family; he represents it to the outside world; he is its mainstay and comfort; he is the master of the house, who exhorts, punishes, helps, and comforts, and stands for it before God. It is a good thing, for it is a divine ordinance when the wife honours the husband for his office's sake, and when the husband properly performs the duties of his office. The husband and wife who acknowledge and observe God's ordinance are 'wise', but those who think to replace it by another of their own devising are 'foolish'.

God has laid on marriage a blessing and a burden. The blessing is the promise of children. God allows man to share in his continual work of creation; but it is always God himself who blesses marriage with children. 'Children are a heritage from the Lord' (Ps. 127.3), and they should be acknowledged as such. It is from God that parents receive their children, and it is to God that they should lead them. Parents therefore have divine authority in respect of their children. Luther speaks of the 'golden chain' with which God invests parents; and scripture adds to the fifth commandment the special promise of long life on earth. Since men live on earth, God has given them a lasting reminder that this earth stands under the curse of sin and is not itself the ultimate reality. Over the destiny of woman and of man lies the dark shadow of a word of God's wrath, a burden from God, which they must carry. The woman must bear her children in pain, and in providing for his family the man must reap many thorns and thistles, and labour in the sweat of his brow. This burden should cause both man and wife to call on God, and should remind them of their eternal destiny in his kingdom. Earthly society is only a beginning of the heavenly society, the earthly home an image of the heavenly home, the earthly family a symbol of the fatherhood of God over all men, for they are his children.

God gives you Christ as the foundation of your marriage. 'Welcome one another, therefore, as Christ has welcomed you, for the glory of God' (Rom. 15). In a word, live together in the forgiveness of your sins, for without it no human fellowship, least of all a marriage, can survive. Don't insist on your rights, don't blame each other, don't judge or condemn each other, don't find fault with each other, but accept each other as you are, and forgive each other every day from the bottom of your hearts.

Your home will be a pastor's home. From it, light and strength will have to go out into many other homes. The pastor undertakes a life of special discipline. The husband must bear alone much that belongs to his ministry, since the ministry is his and must, for the sake of God, be a silent one. So his love for his wife must be all the greater, and he must be all the more concerned to share with her what he may. And as a result the wife will be able to lighten the husband's burden all the more, stand by his side, give him help. As fallible human beings, how can they live and work in Christ's community if they do not persevere in constant prayer and forgiveness, if they do not help each other to live as Christians? The right beginning and daily practice are very important indeed.

From the first day of your wedding till the last the rule must be: 'Welcome one another ... for the glory of God'.

That is God's word for your marriage. Thank him for it; thank him for leading you thus far; ask him to establish your marriage, to confirm it, sanctify it, and preserve it. So your marriage will be 'for the praise of his glory'. Amen.

10

... Today is Ascension Day, and that means that it is a day of great joy for all who can believe that Christ rules the world and our lives. My thoughts go out to all of you, to the church and its services, from which I have now been separated for so long, and also the many unknown people in this building who are bearing their fate in silence. I repeatedly find that these and other thoughts keep me from taking my own little hardships too seriously; that would be very wrong and ungrateful.

I've just written a little more about 'The feeling of time'; I'm very much enjoying it, and when we write from personal experience, we can write more fluently and freely. Thank you very much, father, for Kant's *Anthropologie*, which I've read through; I didn't know it. There was a great deal that was interesting in it, but it has a very rationalist rococo psychology, which simply ignores many essential phenomena. Can you send me something good about forms and functions of memory? It's a thing that interests me very much in this situation. Kant's exposition of 'smoking' as a means of entertaining oneself is very nice...

I read some of Stifter almost every day. The intimate life of his characters – of course it is old-fashioned of him to describe only likeable people – is very pleasant in this atmosphere here, and makes one think of the things that really matter in life. Prison life in general brings one back, both outwardly and inwardly, to the simplest things of life; that explains why I could not get on at all with Rilke. But I wonder whether one's understanding is not affected by the restrictive nature of life here?...

Well, Whitsuntide is here, and we are still separated; but it is in a special way a feast of fellowship. When the bells rang this morning, I longed to go to church, but instead I did as John did on the island of Patmos, and had such a splendid service of my own, that I did not feel lonely at all, for you were all with me, every one of you, and so were the congregations in whose company I have kept Whitsuntide. Every hour or so since yesterday evening I've been repeating to my own comfort Paul Gerhardt's Whitsun hymn with the lovely lines 'Thou art a Spirit of joy' and 'Grant us joyfulness and strength', and besides that, the words 'If you faint in the day of adversity, your strength is small' (Prov. 24), and 'God did not give us a spirit of timidity but a spirit of power and love and self-control' (II Tim. 1). I have again been preoccupied with the strange story of the gift of tongues. That the confusion of tongues at the Tower of Babel, as a result of which people can no longer understand each other, because everyone speaks a different language, should at last be brought to an end and overcome by the language of God, which everyone understands and through which alone people can understand each other again, and that the church should be the place where that happens – these are great momentous thoughts. Leibniz grappled all his life with the idea of a universal script consisting, not of words, but of self-evident signs representing every possible idea. It was an expression of his wish to heal the world, which was then so torn to pieces, a philosophical reflection on the Pentecost story.

Once again all is silent here; one hears nothing but the tramp of the prisoners pacing up and down in their cells. How many comfortless and un-Whitsun-like thoughts there must be in their minds! If I were prison chaplain here, I should spend the whole time from morning till night on days like this, going through the cells; a good deal would happen...

To his parents   24 June 1943

... What a blessing it is, in such distressing times, to belong to a large, closely-knit family, where each trusts the other and stands by them. When pastors were arrested, I sometimes used to think that it must be easiest for those of them who were unattached. But I did not know then what the warmth that radiates from the love of a wife and family can mean in the cold air of imprisonment, and how in just such times of separation the feeling of belonging together through thick and thin actually grows stronger...

Letters from mother and grandmother have just come. Thank you very much. From what you say about strawberries and raspberries, school holidays and plans for travel, I begin to feel that summer has really come. Time is not of much account here. I'm glad the weather is mild. A little while ago a tomtit had its nest with its ten little ones in a recess in the yard here. I enjoyed going to look at it every day till some cruel fellow went and destroyed the lot and left some of the tomtits lying on the ground, dead; I can't understand it. When I walk in the yard I get a great deal of pleasure from a small ant-hill and from the bees in the lime-trees. I sometimes think of the story of Peter Bamm, who was on a lovely island where he met all kinds of people, good and bad. He dreamt in a nightmare that a bomb might come and destroy everything, and the first thing that occurred to him was what a pity it would be for the butterflies! Prison life brings home to one how nature carries on uninterruptedly its quiet, open life, and it gives one quite a special – perhaps a sentimental – attitude towards animal and plant life, except that my attitude towards the flies in my cell remains very unsentimental. In general, a prisoner is no doubt inclined to make up, through an exaggerated sentimentality, for the soullessness and lack of warmth in his surroundings; and perhaps he may react too strongly to anything sentimental that affects him personally. The right thing for him to do then is to call himself to order with a cold shower of common sense and humour, to avoid losing his sense of proportion. I believe it is just here that Christianity, rightly understood, can help particularly...

To his parents   Sunday, 3 July 1943

When the bells of the prison chapel start ringing at about six o'clock on a Saturday evening, that is the best time to write home. It's remarkable what power church bells have over human beings, and how deeply they can affect us. So many of our life's experiences gather round them. All discontent, ingratitude, and selfishness melt away, and in a moment we are left with only our pleasant memories hovering round us like gracious spirits. I always think first of those quiet summer evenings in Friedrichsbrunn, then of all the different parishes that I have worked in, then of all our family occasions, weddings, christenings, and confirmations – tomorrow my godchild is being confirmed! – I really cannot count all the memories that come alive to me, and they all inspire peace, thankfulness, and confidence. If only one could help other people more!...

Just to keep you up to date with things, and not because I think that it's really worth mentioning, I ought to report my lumbago. It's not bad, but it's already lasted more than three weeks; it's a bit of a nuisance. The stone floor is probably the cause. There is everything imaginable here, ray treatment and footbaths, but nothing is any use.

I've now been in prison three months. I remember hearing Schlatter say, in his lectures on ethics, that it was one of the duties of a Christian citizen to take it patiently if he were held for investigation. That meant nothing to me at the time, but in the past few weeks I have thought of it several times, and now we must wait calmly and patiently as long as we have to, just as we have done up to now. I am dreaming more than ever that I have been released and am back home with you.

The day lilies have been simply lovely; their cups open slowly in the morning and bloom only for a day; and the next morning there are fresh ones to take their place. The day after tomorrow they will all be over...

To his parents   Sunday, 24 July 1943

...In my reading I'm now living entirely in the nineteenth century. During these months I've read Gotthelf, Stifter, Immermann, Fontane, and Keller with new admiration. A period in which people could write such clear and simple German must have had quite a healthy core. They treat the most delicate matters without sentimentality, the most serious without flippancy, and they express their convictions without pathos; there is no exaggerated simplifying or complicating of language or subject matter; in short, it's all very much to my liking, and seems to me very sound. But it must have meant plenty of hard work at expressing themselves in good German, and therefore plenty of opportunity for quiet. By the way, the last Reuters were as fascinating as ever; I'm delighted and surprised at their equipoise, which often extends to the language itself. An author's style is often enough to attract or repel the readers...

14

To his parents   3 August 1943

I'm really very happy and thankful that I can write to you oftener now, as I'm afraid you must be worrying about me, first because of the heat in my cell just under the roof, and secondly because of my asking for a lawyer. Your wonderful parcel has just come with tomatoes, apples, bottled fruit, thermos flask, etc., and the cooling salt, which is fantastic – I never knew there was such a thing. What trouble you have taken for me again. Please don't worry; I've often had to put up with worse heat in Italy, Africa, Spain, Mexico, and, almost the worst of all, in New York in July 1939; so I've a fairly good idea what to do about it. I don't eat or drink much, I sit quietly at my desk, and so manage to work unhindered. From time to time I refresh my body and soul with your lovely things. I don't want to ask to be moved to another floor, as that would not be fair to the other prisoner who would have to come into my cell, probably without such things as tomatoes; and besides, it does not make much difference whether the temperature in the cell is 34 or only 30. . .

I've just eaten a couple of the marvellous tomatoes from the garden for my lunch, and thought of the work you've had in picking them. And thank you, father, for your letter. I don't suppose that any one of us loves Friedrichsbrunn less than anyone else. Just think, it's thirty years this year since you bought it. I very much hope for a couple of fine days there with you. Perhaps it will also cure my lumbago. . .

To his parents   17 August 1943

. . . For the last fortnight I've been waiting in such uncertainty day by day that I've hardly felt equal to any serious work; but I'm going to try now to get down to some more writing. Some weeks ago I sketched the outlines of a play, but meanwhile I've realized that the material is not suitable for drama; and so I shall now try to rewrite it as a story. It's about the life of a family, and of course there is a good deal of autobiography mixed up in it.

I would very much like some rough paper and my watch; the other one suddenly stopped yesterday. It's going again now, but it's too risky for me suddenly to be left without a watch. And please could you buy me N. Hartmann's *Systematic Philosophy*? I can now use the personal library here, which has all sorts of good things, so I need less from you. But if you can dig out Stifter's *Witiko*, that would be splendid. – I was very touched when the Schleichers sent me the rabbit liver a little while ago. A real piece of meat is very welcome in all this spoon-fodder; I'm also very grateful to them for biscuits, peaches and cigarettes. Do you by any chance still have a spot of tea? I can occasionally get boiling water...

To his parents   31 August 1943

...For the last few days I've again been able to work well and write a good deal. When I find myself back in the cell after a few hours of complete absorption in my work, it takes me a moment or two to get my bearings again. The fact of my being here is hard to credit even now, however much I get used to the external conditions. I find it quite interesting to watch this gradual process of accustoming and adapting myself. A week ago I was given a knife and fork for my meals – a new provision – and they seemed almost unnecessary, as it had become so much a matter of course for me to use a spoon for spreading my bread and so on. On the other hand, I think there are some things that are so irrational, e.g. the actual state of being in prison, that it is impossible, or at least very difficult, to get used to them. That kind of thing needs a conscious effort if it is to be accepted. I expect there are psychological works on the subject.

Delbrück's *World History* is very good reading, only it seems to me to be more a history of Germany. I've finished *The Microbe Hunters*, and enjoyed it very much. I've also been reading some more of Storm, though without being very much impressed by it on the whole. I hope you will bring me some more of Fontane or Stifter...

To his parents   5 September 1943

I don't think there is any need for us to compare notes about the night before last. I shall never forget looking through the cell window at the horrible night sky. I was very relieved to hear from the Captain the next morning that you were safe. I'm very sorry that Susi has had damage a second time and now has to move house. She also has a load to bear. What a good thing that the children weren't there! And I'm very relieved that Maria does not have to be in Berlin. Wouldn't now be a good time for you at least to spend the nights in Sakrow?

It's remarkable how we think at such times about the people that we should not like to live without, and almost or entirely forget about ourselves. It is only then that we feel how closely our own lives are bound up with other people's, and in fact how the centre of our own lives is outside ourselves, and how little we are separate entities. The 'as though it were a part of me' is perfectly true, as I have often felt after hearing that one of my colleagues or pupils had been killed. I think it is a literal fact of nature that human life extends far beyond our physical existence. Probably a mother feels this more strongly than anyone else. There are two passages in the Bible which always seem to me to sum up this experience. One is from Jeremiah 45: 'Behold, what I have built I am breaking down, and what I have planted I am plucking up ... And do you seek great things for yourself? Seek them not ... but I will give your life as a prize of war ...'; and the other is from Psalm 60: 'Thou hast made the land to quake, thou hast rent it open; repair its breaches, for it totters...'

I'm still getting on all right. I have been moved two floors lower because of the raids, and now it is very nice to have a direct view from my window on to the church towers. Last week I was able to write quite well again. The only thing I miss is open-air exercise, on which I depend very much for any useful work. But it won't be long now, and that is the main thing...

To his parents   13 September 1943

Last time I said I should like to have more letters, and in the last few days I've been delighted to have a whole sheaf of them. I almost seem to be like Palmström, who ordered 'a quarter's mixed correspondence'. But seriously, a day when there are letters is a very noticeable change from the usual monotony. Now that the permission to visit has also come, things really are looking up...

It's a strange feeling to be so completely dependent on other people; but at least it teaches one to be grateful, and I hope I shall

17

never forget that. In ordinary life we hardly realize that we receive a great deal more than we give, and that it is only with gratitude that life becomes rich. It's very easy to overestimate the importance of our own achievements in comparison with what we owe to others.

The stormy happenings in the world in the last few days go right through one, and I wish I could be doing useful service somewhere or other, but at present that 'somewhere' must be in the prison cell, and what I can do here makes its contribution in the unseen world, a sphere where the word 'do' is quite unsuitable. I sometimes think of Schubert's *Münnich* and his crusade.

For the rest, I'm reading and writing as much as I can, and I'm glad to say that I've never had a moment's boredom in the five months and more that I've been here. My time is always fully occupied, but in the background there is always the feeling, from morning till night, of waiting for something. A few weeks ago I asked you to get me some books that have just been published: N. Hartmann's *Systematic Philosophy* and *The Age of Marius and Sulla*; now I should also like *German Music* by R. Benz. I shouldn't like to miss these things, and I should be glad to be able to read them while I am still here. Karl-Friedrich wrote about a book on physics, intended for the general reader, and said he would send it to me. Klaus, too, sometimes discovers books that are worth reading. I've practically finished everything that I want to read here. I may have another try at Jean Paul's *Siebenkäs* or *Flegeljahre*; I have them in my room. I might not bring myself to read them later on, and there are many well-read people who think highly of him. In spite of several attempts, I've always found him too long-winded and affected. But as we're now in mid-September, I hope these wishes will already be out of date before they are fulfilled...

To his parents   4 October 1943

... Outside it's lovely autumn weather, and I wish that you – and I with you – were at Friedrichsbrunn, and also Hans and his family, who are all so specially fond of the cottage. But how many people must there be in the world today who cannot have their wishes met? I certainly don't agree with Diogenes that the greatest happiness is the absence of desire, and that the best place to live in is a

18

tub; why should we be fooled into believing that kind of thing? But I do believe that it may be good for us, especially when we are young, to have to wait for what we want, although we ought not to go so far as to give up wishing for anything and grow apathetic. But I'm in no danger of that at present...

To his parents   13 October 1943

I have in front of me the beautiful bunch of dahlias that you brought me yesterday; it reminds me of the lovely hour that I was able to have with you, and of the garden, and in general of how beautiful the world can be in these autumn days... All that is needed to bring that home to one is a few bright autumn flowers, the view from the cell window, and half an hour's 'exercise' in the prison yard, where there are, in fact, a few beautiful chestnut and lime trees. But in the last resort, for me at any rate, the 'world' consists of a few people whom I should like to see and to be with. The occasional appearances of you and Maria, for a brief hour as though from a great distance, are really the thing for which and from which I principally live. That is contact with my real world. If, besides that, I could sometimes hear a good sermon on Sundays – I sometimes hear fragments of the chorales that are carried along by the breeze – it would be still better...

I've again been doing a good deal of writing lately, and for the work that I have set myself to do, the day is often too short, so that sometimes, comically enough, I even feel that I have 'no time' here for this or that less important matter! After breakfast in the morning (about 7 o'clock) I read some theology, and then I write till midday; in the afternoon I read, then comes a chapter from Delbrück's *World History*, some English grammar, about which I can still learn all kinds of things, and finally, as the mood takes me, I write or read again. Then in the evening I am tired enough to be glad to lie down, though that does not mean going to sleep at once.

When will Maria come to you now? Mother, why don't you simply hand over the housekeeping to her, even if only for a while? It would be a sort of holiday for you, and I imagine that Maria will do it brilliantly. I'm so sorry that you and she have troubled yourselves unnecessarily with the fur. But in the warm white sweater and the ski suit I really feel quite warm, although it's only 12 degrees inside...

To his parents   22 October 1943

... It seems as if my affairs are now beginning to move, and I'm very glad of it; it's all the more unnatural that I can't discuss my concerns with you now, as I used to. But I don't think it can be very much longer now. Anyway, you mustn't suppose that I'm brooding all day on my predicament; that's not so at all, and I think there is no need for it. The last few days and weeks have been quiet, and I've been using them to do as much work as possible; unfortunately I hardly ever do quite as much as I set out to during the day. I've had the great advantage of being able lately to read through undisturbed, and compare with each other, the great German educational and cultural novels, *Wilhelm Meister*, *Der Nachsommer*, *Der Grüne Heinrich*, *Der Hungerpastor* (at present I'm on *Die Flegeljahre*), and I shall enjoy the recollection of them for a long time. I found it very useful, too, to read the *World History*. I still like Hartmann's *Systematic Philosophy* very much; it's a very handy survey. So I can feel as if I had been given a term at a university with a series of good lectures. Of course, any creative output of my own has suffered badly; but I'm now looking forward tremendously to the day when I shall again be in touch, not only with ideas and fictitious figures, but with real people and all our many daily tasks; it will be a very radical change...

To his parents   31 October 1943

... Today is Reformation Day, a feast that in our time can give one plenty to think about. One wonders why Luther's action had to be followed by consequences that were the exact opposite of what he intended, and that darkened the last years of his life, so that he sometimes even doubted the value of his life's work. He wanted a real unity of the church and the West – that is, of the Christian peoples – and the consequence was the disintegration of the church and of Europe; he wanted the 'freedom of the Christian man', and the consequence was indifference and licentiousness; he wanted the establishment of a genuine secular social order free from clerical privilege, and the result was insurrection, the Peasants' War, and soon afterwards the gradual dissolution of all cohesion and order in society. I remember from my student days a discussion between Holl and Harnack as to whether the great historical intellectual and spiritual movements made headway through their primary or their secondary motives. At the time I thought Holl was right in maintaining the former; now I think he was wrong. As long as a hundred years ago Kierkegaard said that today Luther would say the opposite of what he said then. I think he was right – with some reservations. . .

To his parents   9 November 1943

Now the dismal autumn days have begun and one has to try to get light from within. Your letters always help with this; recently they've been coming through with astonishing speed. Once again, your last parcel was particularly fine. I was very surprised and pleased with the Stifter anthology. As it consists mainly of extracts from his letters, it's almost all new to me. My overriding interest for the last ten days has been *Witiko* which, after my giving you so much trouble to hunt for it, was discovered in the library here – a place where I shouldn't really have expected it. Most people would find its thousand pages, which can't be skipped but have to be taken steadily, too much for them, so I'm not sure whether to recommend it to you. For me it's one of the finest books I know. The purity of its style and character-drawing gives one a quite rare and peculiar feeling of happiness. One really ought to read it for the first time at the age of fourteen, instead of the *Kampf um Rom*, and then grow up with it. Even today's good historical novels, e. g. those by Gertrud Bäumer, can't compare with it – it's *sui generis*. I should very much like to own it, but it will hardly be possible to get hold of it. So far, the only historical novels that have made a comparable impression on me are *Don Quixote* and Gotthelf's *Berner Geist*. I've again failed to make anything of Jean Paul; I can't get over the feeling that he is vain and affected. He must have been rather unattractive personally, too. It's fine to go through literature like this on voyages of discovery, and one does discover some quite surprising things, even after so many years' reading. Perhaps you've further suggestions to make?

A few days ago I got Rüdiger's letter, for which I thank him very much. The programme of the Furtwängler concert that he went to did make me wish I could have been there. I hope I won't forget what's left of my technique while I'm here. I sometimes feel a real craving for an evening of music – trio, quartet, or singing; one would like to hear something different from the voices in this building. After more than seven months here one has had more than enough of it. But of course, that's only to be expected, and there is no need to mention it to you. What is not a matter of course is that I'm all right here in spite of everything, that I can experience pleasures of one kind or another, and that with it all I keep my spirits up – and so I'm very thankful every day. Maria is to come on a visit tomorrow. I keep encouraging her along from month to month and ask her to be patient, but it's indescribably difficult for her. . .

To his parents   17 November 1943

While I'm writing this letter, on Repentance Day, the Schleichers, so Ursel told me, are all listening to the B Minor Mass. For years now I've associated it with this particular day, like the St Matthew Passion with Good Friday. I well remember the evening when I first heard it. I was eighteen, and had just come from Harnack's seminar, in which he had discussed my first seminar essay very kindly, and had expressed the hope that some day I should specialize in church history. I was full of this when I went into the Philharmonic Hall; the great *Kyrie Eleison* was just beginning, and as it did so, I forgot everything else – the effect was indescribable. Today I'm going through it, bit by bit, in my mind, and I'm glad the Schleichers can hear it, as it's my favourite work of Bach. . .

To Eberhard Bethge   18 November 1943

As you are in the neighbourhood, I simply must take the opportunity of writing to you. I expect you know that I haven't even been allowed to have the pastor to see me here; but even if he had come – I'm really very glad that I have *only* the Bible – I wouldn't have been able to speak to him in that way which is only possible with you.

You can't imagine how much I worried during the first weeks of my imprisonment in case your wedding plans didn't come off. I prayed a great deal for you and Renate, and thanked God for every day on which I had good news of you. Your wedding day *really* was a day of joy for me, like few others. Later in September it was a great torment not to be able to support you. But the certainty that so far you have been guided with such unbelievable friendship made me quite confident that God intends things to be very well with you...

And now, after these long months without worship, penitence and eucharist and without the *consolatio fratrum* – once again be my pastor as you have so often been in the past, and listen to me. There is so infinitely much to report, that I would like to tell both of you, but today it can only be the essentials, so this letter is for you alone ... So let me tell you a little that you ought to know about me. For the first twelve days, during which I was segregated and treated as a felon – up to now the cells on each side of me have been occupied almost solely by fettered men awaiting death – Paul Gerhardt was an unexpectedly helpful standby, and so were the Psalms and Revelation. During this time I have been preserved from any serious spiritual trial. You are the only person who knows how often *accidie, tristitia*, with all its menacing consequences, has lain in wait for me; and I feared at the time that you must be worrying about me on that account. But I told myself from the beginning that I was not going to oblige either man or devil in any such way – they can do what they like about it for themselves; and I hope I shall always be able to stand firm on this.

At first I wondered a good deal whether it was really for the cause of Christ that I was causing you all such grief; but I soon put that out of my head as a temptation, as I became certain that the duty had been laid on me to hold out in this boundary situation with all its problems; I became quite content to do this, and have remained so ever since (I Peter 2.20; 3.14).

I've reproached myself for not having finished my *Ethics* (parts of it have probably been confiscated), and it was some consolation to me that I have told you the essentials, and that even if you had forgotten it, it would probably emerge again indirectly somehow. Besides, my ideas were still incomplete.

I also felt it to be an omission not to have carried out my long-cherished wish to attend the Lord's Supper once again with you. I wanted to tell you once again how grateful I am that you ... bore with such patience and tolerance all the things with which I have sometimes made life hard for you. I ask you for forgiveness, and yet I know that we have shared spiritually, even if not physically, in the gift of confession, absolution, and communion, and that we may be quite happy and easy in our minds about it. But I did just want to tell you this.

As soon as it was possible, apart from my daily work on the Bible (I've read through the Old Testament two and a half times and learnt a great deal), I began to do some non-theological work. An essay on 'The feeling of time' originated mainly in the need to bring before me my own past in a situation in which time could so easily seem 'empty' and 'lost'. Our past is always kept before us by thankfulness and penitence. But more of that later.

Then I started on a bold enterprise that I've had in mind for a long time; I began to write the story of a contemporary middle-class family. The background for this consisted of all our in-numerable conversations on the subject, and my own personal experiences; in short, it was to rehabilitate middle-class life as we know it in our own families, and especially in the light of Christianity. It tells of two families on terms of friendship living in a small town. Their children grow up, and as they gradually enter into the responsibilities of official positions, they try to work together for the good of the community as mayor, teacher, pastor, doctor, engineer. You would recognize many familiar features, and you come into it too. But I haven't yet got much further than the beginning, mainly because the repeated false forecasts of my release have made it difficult for me to concentrate. But the work is giving me great pleasure. Only I wish I could talk it over with you every day; indeed, I miss that more than you think. I may often have originated our ideas, but the clarification of them was com-pletely on your side. I only learnt in conversation with you whether an idea was any good or not. I long to read to you some of what I've written. Your comments on details are so much better than mine. Perhaps that seems to be mad presumption?!

Incidentally, I've written an essay on 'What is "speaking the truth"?', and at the moment I'm trying to write some prayers for

24

prisoners; it's surprising that there are none, and perhaps these may be distributed at Christmas.

And now for my reading. Yes, Eberhard, I'm very sorry that we did not get to know Stifter together; it would have helped us very much in our talks, but we shall have to put it off till later. But I've a great deal to tell you about that. Later? When and how will it come about? To be on the safe side, I've made my will and given it to my lawyer. In it, I've left almost everything I have to you. But first Maria must be allowed to look for something that she would like in remembrance. If this should happen, please be very good to Maria, and if possible, write to her in my stead from time to time, just a few kind words, as you can do so well, and tell her gently that I asked you to. But perhaps – or certainly – you are now going into greater danger. I shall be thinking of you every day and asking God to protect you and bring you back. Please take with you anything of mine that you need; I'm only too pleased to know it's with you. And please provide yourself with as much of the food that has come for me as you need. That's a thought that would comfort me very much.

There is so much that I would very, very much like to hear of you. Sometimes I've thought that it is really very good for the two of you that I'm not there. At the beginning it's not at all easy to resolve the conflict between marriage and friendship; you're spared this problem, and later it won't exist. But that's only a private and passing thought; you mustn't laugh at it.

I wonder whether, if I'm not condemned, but released and called up, it might be arranged for me to get to your neighbourhood. That would be fine! Anyway, if I should be condemned (one never knows), don't worry about me. It really doesn't worry me at all, except that in that case I shall probably be kept here for a few more months longer 'on probation', and that's really not pleasant. But there is a great deal that isn't pleasant! The thing for which I should be condemned is so unexceptionable that I should only be proud of it. But I hope that, if God preserves us, we shall at least be able to celebrate Easter happily together. And then, *sub conditione Jacobea*, I shall baptize your child!

And now, Eberhard, good-bye. I don't expect a long letter from you. You've little time now. But let's promise to remain faithful in interceding for each other. I shall ask that you may have strength, health, patience, and protection from conflicts and temptations. You can ask for the same things for me. And if it should be decided that we are not to meet again, let us remember each other to the end in thankfulness and forgiveness, and may God grant us that one day we may stand before his throne praying for each other and joining in praise and thankfulness...

... By the way, I've heard that Warsaw is frightfully dear. Take as much as you can with you; if you need money, feel free to draw 1000 marks of mine. I can't use it. Do you always get my letters to my parents to read? See that they send them to you. I'm finding here (I expect you are, too) that the most difficult thing is getting up in the morning (Jer. 31.26!). I'm now praying quite simply for freedom. There is such a thing as a false composure which is quite unchristian. As Christians, we needn't be at all ashamed of some impatience, longing, opposition to what is unnatural, and our full share of desire for freedom, earthly happiness, and opportunity for effective work. I think we entirely agree about that.

Well, in spite of everything, or rather because of everything, that we are now going through, each in his own way, we shall still be the same as before, shan't we? I hope you don't think I am here turning out to be a 'man of the inner line'; I was never in less danger of that, and I think the same applies to you. What a happy day it will be when we tell each other our experiences. But I sometimes get very angry at not being free yet!

My wedding plans: if I am free and still have at least a couple of months before I'm called up, I want to get married. If I have only two or three weeks free before the call-up, then I want to wait until the end of the war. What an engagement we're having! Maria is astounding! You don't think that's too much to ask? If only we had seen each other at least a couple of times in January! I don't know why Maria has to put up with so much hardship, young as she is. I hope that it isn't too much for her, but I'm so glad to have her now. Or do you think that it would have been better and more unselfish if I had asked her after my arrest simply to wait for my release without letters and visits? I would have regarded that as un-natural, and I think that you would have done, too. Please think of her, too, when you think of me...

... A little more about my daily routine: We get up at the same time, and the day lasts till 8 p.m.; I wear out my trousers by sitting while you wear out your soles by walking. I read the *Völkischer Beobachter* and the *Reich*, and I've got to know several *very* nice people. Every day I'm taken for half an hour's walking alone, and in the afternoon they give me treatment in the sick-bay – very kindly, but unsuccessfully – for my rheumatism. Every week I get from you the most marvellous things to eat. Thank you very much for everything, and also for the cigars and cigarettes that you sent me while you were away. I only hope you have plenty to eat – do you get very hungry? That would be horrid. There is nothing I miss here – except all of you. I wish I could play the G minor sonata with you and sing some Schütz, and hear you sing Psalms 70 and 47; that was what you did best.

My cell is being cleaned out for me, and while it's being done, I can give the cleaner something to eat. One of them was sentenced to death the other day; it affected me a lot. One sees a great deal in seven and a half months, particularly what heavy consequences may follow trivial acts of folly. I think a lengthy confinement is demoralizing in *every* way for most people. I've been thinking out an alternative penal system on the principle of making the punishment fit the crime; e.g., for absence without leave, the cancelling of leave; for unauthorized wearing of medals, longer service at the front; for robbing other soldiers, the temporary labelling of a man as a thief; for dealing in the black market, a reduction of rations; and so on. Why does the Old Testament law never punish anyone by depriving him of his freedom? ...

21 November

Today is Remembrance Sunday ... Then comes Advent, with all its happy memories for us. It was you who really first opened up to me the world of music-making that we have carried on during the weeks of Advent. Life in a prison cell may well be compared to Advent; one waits, hopes, and does this, that, or the other – things that are really of no consequence – the door is shut, and can be opened only *from the outside*. That idea is just as it occurs to me;

don't suppose we go in very much for symbolism here! But I must tell you two other things that may surprise you: First, I very much miss meal-time fellowship. Everything that I get from you for my material enjoyment becomes here a reminder of my table-fellowship with you. So may not this be an essential part of life, because it is a reality of the Kingdom of God? Secondly, I've found that following Luther's instruction to 'make the sign of the cross' at our morning and evening prayers is in itself helpful. There is something objective about it, and that is what is particularly badly needed here. Don't be alarmed; I shall not come out of here a *homo religiosus*! On the contrary, my fear and distrust of 'religiosity' have become greater than ever here. The fact that the Israelites *never* uttered the name of God always makes me think, and I can understand it better as I go on. . .

I'm now reading a lot of Tertullian, Cyprian, and other church fathers with interest. In some ways they are more relevant to our time than the Reformers, and at the same time they provide a basis for talks between Protestants and Roman Catholics.

Do you sometimes wonder why I allow so much food to be sent when I know well enough that you yourselves are short? To begin with, during the months of interrogation I thought it important to keep my strength for the sake of the cause. Later, people kept holding out the prospect of an early ending, and I wanted to keep in physical trim as much as possible for that. The same thing applies again now. Once I'm free or condemned, of course, it will stop. Anyway, I believe that on purely legal grounds my condemnation is out of the question.

Prayers for Fellow-Prisoners
Christmas 1943

MORNING PRAYER

O God, early in the morning I cry to you.
Help me to pray
And to concentrate my thoughts on you;
I cannot do this alone.

In me there is darkness,
But with you there is light;
I am lonely, but you do not leave me;
I am feeble in heart, but with you there is help;
I am restless, but with you there is peace.
In me there is bitterness, but with you there is patience;
I do not understand your ways,
But you know the way for me.

O heavenly Father,
I praise and thank you
For rest in the night;
I praise and thank you for this new day;
I praise and thank you for all your goodness
and faithfulness throughout my life.

You have granted me many blessings;
Now let me also accept what is hard
from your hand.
You will lay on me no more
than I can bear.
You make all things work together for good
for your children.

Lord Jesus Christ,
You were poor
and in distress, a captive and forsaken as I am.
You know all man's troubles;
You abide with me
when all men fail me;
You remember and seek me;
It is your will that I should know you
and turn to you.
Lord, I hear your call and follow;
Help me.

O Holy Spirit,
Give me faith that will protect me
from despair, from passions, and from vice;

Give me such love for God and men
as will blot out all hatred and bitterness;
Give me the hope that will deliver me
from fear and faint-heartedness.

O holy and merciful God,
my Creator and Redeemer,
my Judge and Saviour,
You know me and all that I do.
You hate and punish evil without respect of persons
in this world and the next;
You forgive the sins of those
who sincerely pray for forgiveness;
You love goodness, and reward it on this earth
with a clear conscience,
and, in the world to come,
with a crown of righteousness.

I remember in your presence all my loved ones,
my fellow-prisoners, and all who in this house
perform their hard service;
Lord, have mercy.
Restore me to liberty,
and enable me so to live now
that I may answer before you and before men.
Lord, whatever this day may bring,
Your name be praised.
Amen.

In my sleep he watches yearning
and restores my soul,
so that each recurring morning
love and goodness make me whole.
Were God not there,
his face not near,
He had not led me out of fear.
All things have their time and sphere:
God's love lasts for ever.

Paul Gerhardt

EVENING PRAYER

O Lord my God, thank you
for bringing this day to a close;
Thank you for giving me rest
in body and soul.
Your hand has been over me
and has guarded and preserved me.
Forgive my lack of faith
and any wrong that I have done today,
and help me to forgive all who have wronged me.

Let me sleep in peace under your protection,
and keep me from all the temptations of darkness.

Into your hands I commend my loved ones
and all who dwell in this house;
I commend to you my body and soul.
O God, your holy name be praised.
Amen.

Each day tells the other
my life is but a journey
to great and endless life.
O sweetness of eternity,
may my heart grow to love thee;
my home is not in time's strife.

Tersteegen

PRAYER IN TIME OF DISTRESS

O Lord God,
great distress has come upon me;
and I do not know what to do.
O God, be gracious to me and help me.
Give me strength to bear what you send,
and do not let fear rule over me;
Take a father's care of those I love,
My wife and children.

31

O merciful God,
forgive me all the sins that I have committed
against you and against my fellow men.
I trust in your grace
and commit my life wholly into your hands.
Do with me according to your will
and as is best for me.
Whether I live or die, I am with you,
and you, my God, are with me.
Lord, I wait for your salvation
and for your kingdom.
Amen.

Every Christian in his place
    should be brave and free,
with the world face to face.
Though death strikes, his spirit should
    persevere, without fear
    calm and good.
For death cannot destroy,
but from grief brings relief
    and opens gates to joy.
Closed the door of bitter pain,
    bright the way where we may
    all heaven gain.

Paul Gerhardt

To Eberhard Bethge   Friday, 26 November 1943

So it really came off! Only for a moment, but that doesn't matter so
much; even a few hours would be far too little, and when we are
isolated here we can take in so much that even a few minutes gives
us something to think about for a long time afterwards. It will be
with me for a long time now – the memory of having the four
people who are nearest and dearest to me with me for a brief
moment. When I got back to my cell afterwards, I paced up and
down for a whole hour, while my dinner stood there and got cold,
so that at last I couldn't help laughing at myself when I found

myself repeating over and over again, 'That was really great!' I always hesitate to use the word 'indescribable' – but at the moment that is just what this morning seems to be. Karl [Barth]'s cigar is on the table in front of me, and that is something really indescribable – was he nice? and understanding? and V[isser 't Hooft] too? How grand it was that you saw them. And the good old favourite 'Wolf' cigar from Hamburg, which I used to be so fond of in better times. Just by me, standing on a box, is Maria's Advent garland, and on the shelf there are (among other things) your gigantic eggs, waiting for breakfasts still to come. (It's no use my saying that you oughtn't to have deprived yourselves of them; but that's what I think, though I am glad of them all the same.)...

Now you've been able to convince yourself that I'm my old self in every respect and that all is well. I believe that a moment was enough to make clear to both of us that everything that has happened in the last seven and a half months has left both of us essentially unchanged; I never doubted it for a moment, and you certainly didn't either. That's the advantage of having spent almost every day and having experienced almost every event and discussed every thought together for eight years. One needs only a second to know about each other, and now one doesn't really need even that second any more. I can remember that my first visit to a prison (I went to see Fritz O., and you were with me) took it out of me terribly, although Fritz was very cheerful and nice. I hope you didn't feel like that when you were here today. You see, it would be wrong to suppose that prison life is uninterrupted torture. It certainly is not, and visits like yours relieve it for days on end, even though they do, of course, awaken feelings that have fortunately lain dormant for a while. But that doesn't matter either. I realize again in thankfulness how well off I was, and feel new hope and energy. Thank you *very* much, you yourself and all the others...

27 November

Meanwhile we've had the expected large-scale attack on Borsig. It really is a strange feeling, to see the 'Christmas trees', the flares that the leading aircraft drops, coming down right over our heads. The shouting and screaming of the prisoners in their cells was terrible. We had no dead, only injured, and we had finished bandaging them by one o'clock. After that, I was able to drop off at once into a sound sleep. People here talk quite openly about how frightened they were. I don't quite know what to make of it, for fright is surely something to be ashamed of. I have a feeling that it shouldn't be talked about except in the confessional, otherwise it might easily involve a certain amount of exhibitionism; and *a fortiori* there is no need to play the hero. On the other hand, naïve frankness can be quite disarming. But even so, there's a cynical, I might almost say ungodly, frankness, the kind that breaks out in heavy drinking and fornication, and gives the impression of chaos. I wonder whether fright is not one of the *pudenda*, which ought to be concealed. I must think about it further; you've no doubt had your own experiences of it.

The fact that the horrors of war are now coming home to us with such force will no doubt, if we survive, provide us with the necessary basis for making it possible to reconstruct the life of the nations, both spiritually and materially, on Christian principles. So we must really keep these experiences intact, meditate on them, make them bear fruit, and not just shake them off. Never have we been so plainly conscious of the wrath of God, and that is a sign of his grace: 'O that today you would hearken to his voice! Harden not your hearts.' The tasks that confront us are immense, but we must prepare ourselves for them now and be ready when they come...

28 November, Advent I

It began with a peaceful night. When I was in bed yesterday evening I looked up for the first time 'our' Advent hymns in the *Neues Lied*. I can hardly hum any of them to myself without being reminded of Finkenwalde, Schlönwitz, and Sigurdshof. Early this morning I held my Sunday service, hung up the Advent garland on a nail, and fastened Lippi's picture of the Nativity in the middle of it. At breakfast I greatly enjoyed the second of your ostrich eggs. Soon after that, I was taken to the sick-bay for a discussion which lasted till noon. The last air raid brought some most unpleasant experiences – a land-mine 25 metres away; a sick-bay with no lights or windows, prisoners screaming for help, with no one but ourselves taking any notice of them; but we too could do very little to help in the darkness, and one has to be cautious about opening the cell doors of those with the heaviest sentences, for you never know whether they will hit you on the head with a chair leg and try to get away. In short, it was not very nice. As a result, I wrote a report of what had taken place, pointing out the need of medical attention during air raids. I hope it will be some use. I'm glad to be able to help in any way with reasonable suggestions.

By the way, I forgot to tell you that I smoked the fabulously fragrant 'Wolf' cigar yesterday afternoon during a pleasant conversation in the sick-bay. Thank you very much for it. Since the raids started, the cigarette situation has unfortunately become calamitous.

While the injured people were being bandaged, they asked for a cigarette, and the medical orderlies and I had already used up a lot beforehand; so I'm all the more grateful for what you brought me the day before yesterday. Nearly every window in the place has been blown out, and the men are sitting in their cells freezing. Although I had forgotten to open my windows when I left the cell, I found at night to my great surprise that they were undamaged. I'm very glad about that, although I'm terribly sorry for the others.

How good it is that you can be at home to celebrate Advent. Just now you will be singing the first hymns together. It makes me think of Altdorfer's 'Nativity' and the verse

> *The crib now glistens bright and clear,*
> *The night brings in a new light here;*
> *The darkness, conquered, fades away,*
> *For faith within the light must stay.*

and also the Advent melody

though not in four-four time, but in a flowing expectant rhythm to suit the text. After this I'm going to read another of W. H. Riehl's entertaining stories. You would enjoy them, too, and they would do very well for reading aloud to the family. You must try to get hold of them some time.

Unfortunately I'm not on the same wavelength as Maria yet in the literary sphere. She writes me such good, natural letters, but she reads ... Rilke, Bergengruen, Binding, Wiechert; I regard the last three as being below our level and the first as being decidedly unhealthy. And in fact they don't really suit her at all ... We ought to be able to talk to each other about such things, and I don't know whether they are altogether unimportant. I would very much like my wife to be as much of the same mind as possible in such questions. But I think it's only a matter of time. I don't like it when husbands and wives have different opinions. They must stand together like an impregnable bulwark. Don't you think so? Or is that another aspect of my 'tyrannical' nature that you know so well? If so, you must tell me. The difference in our ages probably also makes itself felt in these literary matters. Unfortunately the generation of Maria and Renate has grown up with a very bad kind of contemporary literature and finds it much harder than we did to take up earlier writing. The more we have come up against the really good things, the more insipid the weak lemonade of more recent productions has become to us, sometimes almost to the point of making us ill. Can you think of a book from the belles-lettres of, say, the last fifteen years which you think has lasting value? I can't. It is partly just talk, partly striking attitudes, partly plaintive sentimentality – no insight, no ideas, no clarity, no substance and almost always bad unfree writing. At this point I am quite determinedly a *laudator temporis acti*. Are you?

29 November

Today is quite different from all the previous Mondays. Usually on Monday mornings the shouting and swearing in the corridors is at its fiercest, but after the experiences of last week even the loudest shouters and bullies have become quite subdued – a most obvious change.

Now there's something I must tell you personally: the heavy air raids, especially the last one, when the windows of the sick-bay were blown out by the land mine, and bottles and medical supplies fell down from the cupboards and shelves, and I lay on the floor in the darkness with little hope of coming through the attack safely, led me back quite simply to prayer and the Bible. More about that

36

later when I see you. In more than one respect my time of imprisonment is being a very wholesome though drastic cure. But the details must wait till I can tell you personally...

Tuesday, 30 November

... In the months that have passed I've learnt as never before that I owe all the alleviations and help that I get here, not to myself, but to others. On earlier occasions I've felt that you suffer somewhat under the thought that you also owe much in your life to other men. But that is quite perverse. The wish to be independent in everything is false pride. Even what we owe to others belongs to ourselves and is a part of our own lives, and any attempt to calculate what we have 'earned' for ourselves and what we owe to other people is certainly not Christian, and is, moreover, a futile undertaking. It's through what he himself is, plus what he receives that a man becomes a complete entity. I wanted to tell you this because I've now experienced it for myself, though not for the first time, for it was already implicit all through the years of our *vita communis*. I've certainly not received less from you than you from me.

To his parents   Advent I, 28 November 1943

Although I don't know whether and how letters are getting through at present, I want to write to you on the afternoon of the First Sunday in Advent. Altdorfer's 'Nativity' is very topical this year, showing the Holy Family and the crib among the ruins of a tumbledown house. However did he come to paint like that, against all tradition, four hundred years ago? Perhaps he meant that Christmas could and should be kept even in such conditions; in any case, that is his message for us. I like to think of your sitting with the children and keeping Advent with them, just as you used to years ago with us. Only we do everything more intensively now, as we don't know how much longer we have...

These last few days, I have been enjoying W. H. Riehl's *Stories from Olden Times*. You may remember the book from a much earlier period. Today it's just about forgotten, though it is still very pleasant and enjoyable reading; it would also be suitable for reading

37

aloud to the children. As far as I can remember, we had a few of his works at home, but we've probably given them away since then to some collection or other.

It would be very nice if you could bring me the book on superstition. They are starting to consult cards here about the chances of a raid during the coming night. It's interesting how superstition thrives in unsettled times, and how many are prepared to listen to it, at least with half an ear...

To Eberhard Bethge   Advent II [5 December 1943]

... My thoughts and feelings seem to be getting more and more like those of the Old Testament, and in recent months I have been reading the Old Testament much more than the New. It is only when one knows the unutterability of the name of God that one can utter the name of Jesus Christ; it is only when one loves life and the earth so much that without them everything seems to be over that one may believe in the resurrection and a new world; it is only when one submits to God's law that one may speak of grace; and it is only when God's wrath and vengeance are hanging as grim realities over the heads of one's enemies that something of what it means to love and forgive them can touch our hearts. In my opinion it is not Christian to want to take our thoughts and feelings too quickly and too directly from the New Testament. We have already talked about this several times, and every day confirms my opinion. One cannot and must not speak the last word before the last but one. We live in the last but one and believe the last, don't we? Lutherans (so-called!) and pietists would shudder at the thought, but it is true all the same. In *The Cost of Discipleship* (ch. 1) I just hinted at this, but did not follow it up; I must do so later. But the logical conclusions are far-reaching, e.g. for the problem of Catholicism, for the concept of the ministry, for the use of the Bible, etc., and above all for ethics. Why is it that in the Old Testament men tell lies vigorously and often to the glory of God (I've now collected the passages), kill, deceive, rob, divorce, and even fornicate (see the genealogy of Jesus), doubt, blaspheme, and curse, whereas in the New Testament there is nothing of all this? 'An earlier stage' of religion? That is a very naïve way out; it is one and the same God. But more of this later when we meet.

Meanwhile evening has come. The NCO who has just brought me from the sick-bay to my quarters said to me as he left, with an embarrassed smile but quite seriously, 'Pray for us, Pastor, that we may have no alert tonight.'...

For some time I've been taking my daily walk with a man who has been a District Orator, Regional Leader, Government Director, former member of the governing body of the German-Christian Church in Brunswick, and is at present a Party Leader in Warsaw. He has completely gone to pieces here, and clings to me just like a child, consulting me about every little thing, telling me whenever he has cried, etc. After being very cool with him for several weeks, I'm now able to ease things for him a little; his gratitude is quite touching, and he tells me again and again how glad he is to have met a man like me here. Well, the strangest situations do come about; if only I could tell you properly about them!

I've been thinking again over what I wrote to you recently about our own fear. I think that here, under the guise of honesty, something is being passed off as 'natural' that is at bottom a symptom of sin; it is really quite analogous to talking openly about sexual matters. After all, 'truthfulness' does not mean uncovering everything that exists. God himself made clothes for men; and that means that *in statu corruptionis* many things in human life ought to remain covered, and that evil, even though it cannot be eradicated, ought at least to be concealed. Exposure is cynical, and although the cynic prides himself on his exceptional honesty, or claims to want truth at all costs, he misses the crucial fact that since the fall there must be reticence and secrecy. In my opinion the greatness of Stifter lies in his refusal to force his way into man's inner life, in his respect for reticence, and in his willingness to observe people more or less cautiously from the outside but not from the inside. Inquisitiveness is alien to him. I remember once being impressed when Frau von Kleist-Kieckow told me with genuine horror about a film that showed the growth of a plant speeded up; she said that she and her husband could not stand it, as they felt it to be an impermissible prying into the mystery of life. Stifter takes a similar line. But is not this somewhat akin to the so-called English 'hypocrisy', which we contrast with German 'honesty'? I believe we Germans have never properly grasped the meaning of 'conceal-ment', i.e. what is in the end the *status corruptionis* of the world.

39

Kant says quite rightly in his *Anthropologie* that anyone who mis-understands or questions the significance of outward appearance in the world is a traitor to humanity... 'Speaking the truth' (on which I have written an essay) means, in my opinion, saying how something really is – that is, showing respect for secrecy, intimacy, and concealment. 'Betrayal', for example, is not truth, any more than are flippancy, cynicism, etc. What is secret may be revealed only in the confessional, i.e. in the presence of God. More about that later, too.

There are two ways of dealing psychologically with adversities. One way, the easier, is to try to ignore them; that is about as far as I have got. The other and more difficult way is to face them deliber-ately and overcome them; I'm not equal to that yet, but one must learn to do it, for the first way is a slight, though, I believe, a permissible, piece of self-deception.

To Eberhard Bethge   15 December 1943

When I read your letter yesterday, I felt as though a spring, without which my intellectual life was beginning to dry up, had begun once again to produce the first drops of water for a long, long time. Of course, that may sound an exaggeration to you; for first, in the meantime another spring has opened up for you, and moreover, you have many possibilities of replenishment. In my isolation things are quite different. I am forced to live from the past; the future which announces itself in the person of Maria still consists so very much of hints that it lies more on the horizon of hope than in the realm of possession and tangible experience. In any case, your letter set my thoughts going again, after they had grown rusty and tired during recent weeks. I had become so used to talking everything over with you that the sudden and prolonged interruption meant a profound change and a great deprivation. Now we're at least in touch again...

And now I'm taking up with great pleasure your 'fireside chat' (appropriately enough the electricity has failed again, and I'm using candles). So I imagine the two of us sitting together as we used to in the old days after supper (and after our regular evening's 'work') in my room upstairs, smoking, occasionally strumming chords on the clavichord, and discussing the day's events. I should have no end of questions to ask you, about your training, about your journey to Karolus ... And then at last I should have to start telling you that, in spite of everything that I've written so far, things here are revolting, that my grim experiences often pursue me into the night and that I can shake them off only by reciting one hymn after another, and that I'm apt to wake up with a sigh rather than with a hymn of praise to God. It's possible to get used to physical hardships, and to live for months out of the body, so to speak – almost too much so – but one doesn't get used to the psychological strain; on the contrary, I have the feeling that everything that I see and hear is putting years on me, and I'm often finding the world nauseating and burdensome. You're probably surprised now at my talking like this after all my letters; you wrote very kindly that I was making 'something of an effort' to reassure you about my situation. I often wonder who I really am – the man who goes on squirming under these ghastly experiences in wretchedness that cries to heaven, or the man who scourges himself and pretends to others (and even to himself) that he is placid, cheerful, composed, and in control of himself, and allows people to admire him for it (i.e. for playing the part – or is it not playing a part?). What does one's attitude mean, anyway? In short, I know less than ever about myself, and I'm no longer attaching any importance to it. I've had more than enough psychology, and I'm less and less inclined to analyse the state of my soul. That is why I value Stifter and Gotthelf so much. There is something more at stake than self-knowledge.

Then I should discuss with you whether you think that this process, which has associated me with the *Abwehr* (I hardly think that has remained a secret), may prevent me from taking up my ministry again later on. At present you're the only person with whom I can discuss this question, and perhaps we shall be able to talk it over together if you're allowed to see me. Please think it over, and tell me the truth.

Finally, I couldn't talk about anything else with you but Maria. We've now been engaged almost a year, and so far we haven't spent even an hour alone together. Isn't that mad! ... We have to talk and write about things which in the end aren't the most important for the two of us; every month we sit primly for an hour, side by side, as on a school bench, and then we're torn apart again ... Isn't that an impossible situation? And she bears up with such great self-control. It's only occasionally that something else comes through, as on the last visit, when I told her that even Christmas wasn't certain yet. She sighed and said, 'Oh, that will be *too* long for me.' I know that she won't leave me in the lurch; it isn't 'too long' for her self-possession, but for her heart, and that's much more important. The only thing that I keep saying to myself is that it has all come about without our doing and so will probably make sense one day. As long as I don't do her wrong by asking too much of her...

I sometimes feel as if my life were more or less over, and as if all I had to do now were to finish my *Ethics*. But, you know, when I feel like this, there comes over me a longing (unlike any other that I experience) to have a child and not to vanish without trace – an Old Testament rather than a New Testament wish, I suppose ... Yes, I would tell you all this and much more, and would know that (provided that you weren't reading a newspaper or dropping off or even thinking of Renate!) you would listen to me like no one else and would give me good counsel. It may be that all my problems will blow away the moment I'm released – I hope so! Perhaps you can write me a few more words about my questions and my thoughts.

If only we could meet in freedom before you leave! But if they really intend to keep me here over Christmas, I shall keep it in my own way as a Christmas at the front, so you can have an easy mind about it. Great battles are easier to fight and less wearing than the daily guerrilla war. And I do hope you will somehow or other manage to wangle a few days' leave in February; I shall certainly be out of here by then for, to judge by the nonsense that they're bringing against me, they're bound to let me out after the trial.

I'm again working at my essay on 'What is "speaking the truth"?' I'm trying to draw a sharp contrast between trust, loyalty, and secrecy on the one hand, and the 'cynical' conception of truth, for which all these obligations do not exist, on the other. 'Falsehood' is the destruction of, and hostility to, reality as it is in God; anyone who tells the truth cynically is lying. By the way, it's remarkable how little I miss going to church. I wonder why...

42

There's probably nothing for it but to write you a Christmas letter now to meet all eventualities. Although it passes my comprehension that they may possibly still keep me here over Christmas, I've learnt in the past eight and a half months that the unexpected often happens, and that what can't be changed must be accepted with a *sacrificium intellectus*, although the *sacrificium* is not quite complete, and the *intellectus* silently goes its own way.

Above all, you mustn't think that I'm going to let myself be depressed by this lonely Christmas; it will always take its special place among the other unusual Christmases that I've kept in Spain, America, and England, and I want in later years to look back on the time here, not with shame, but with a certain pride. That's the only thing that no one can take from me.

Of course, you, Maria and the family and friends, can't help thinking of my being in prison over Christmas, and it's bound to cast a shadow over the few happy hours that are left to you in these times. The only thing I can do to help is to believe and know that your thoughts about it will be the same as mine, and that we shall be at one in our attitude towards the keeping of this Christmas. Indeed, it can't be otherwise, for that attitude is simply a spiritual inheritance from you. I needn't tell you how I long to be released and to see you all again. But for years you have given us such perfectly lovely Christmases that our grateful recollection of them is strong enough to put a darker one into the background. It's not till such times as these that we realize what it means to possess a past and a spiritual inheritance independent of changes of time and circumstance. The consciousness of being borne up by a spiritual tradition that goes back for centuries gives one a feeling of confidence and security in the face of all passing strains and stresses. I believe that anyone who is aware of such reserves of strength needn't be ashamed of more tender feelings evoked by the memory of a rich and noble past, for in my opinion they belong to the better and nobler part of mankind. They will not overwhelm those who hold fast to values that no one can take from them.

From the Christian point of view there is no special problem about Christmas in a prison cell. For many people in this building it will probably be a more sincere and genuine occasion than in places where nothing but the name is kept. That misery, suffering,

43

poverty, loneliness, helplessness, and guilt mean something quite different in the eyes of God from what they mean in the judgment of man, that God will approach where men turn away, that Christ was born in a stable because there was no room for him in the inn – these are things that a prisoner can understand better than other people; for him they really are glad tidings, and that faith gives him a part in the communion of saints, a Christian fellowship breaking the bounds of time and space and reducing the months of confinement here to insignificance...

To Eberhard Bethge   18 December 1943

You too must at least have a letter for Christmas. I'm no longer expecting to be released. As far as I could see, I should have been released on 17 December, but the lawyers wanted to take the safe course, and now I shall probably be kept here for weeks if not months. The past weeks have been more of a strain than anything before that. There's no changing things now, but it's more difficult to adapt oneself to something that one thinks could have been prevented than to something inevitable. But when facts have taken shape, one just has to fit in with them. What I'm thinking of particularly today is that you too will soon be facing facts that will be very hard for you, probably even harder than for me. I now think that we ought first of all to do everything we can to change those facts while there's still time; and then, if we've tried everything, even though it has been in vain, they will be much easier to bear. Of course, not everything that happens is simply 'God's will'; yet in the last resort nothing happens 'without God's will' (Matt. 10.29), i.e. through every event, however untoward, there is access to God. When a man enters on a supremely happy marriage and has thanked God for it, it is a terrible blow to discover that the same God who established the marriage now demands of us a period of such great deprivation. In my experience nothing tortures us more than longing. Some people have been so violently shaken in their lives from their earliest days that they cannot now, so to speak, allow themselves any great longing or put up with a long period of tension, and they find compensation in short-lived pleasures that offer readier satisfaction. That is the fate of the proletarian classes, and it is the ruin of all intellectual fertility. It's

44

not true to say that it is good for a man to have suffered heavy blows early and often in life; in most cases it breaks him. True, it hardens people for times like ours, but it also greatly helps to deaden them. When *we* are forcibly separated for any considerable time from those whom we love, we simply *cannot*, as most can, get some cheap substitute through other people – I don't mean because of moral considerations, but just because we are what we are. Substitutes repel us; we simply have to wait and wait; we have to suffer unspeakably from the separation, and feel the longing till it almost makes us ill. That is the only way, although it is a very painful one, in which we can preserve unimpaired our relationship with our loved ones. A few times in my life I've come to know what homesickness means. There is nothing more painful, and during these months in prison I've sometimes been terribly homesick. And as I expect you will have to go through the same kind of thing in the coming months, I wanted to write and tell you what I've learnt about it, in case it may be of some help to you. The first result of such longing is always a wish to neglect the ordinary daily routine in some way or other, and that means that our lives become disordered. I used to be tempted sometimes to stay in bed after six in the morning (it would have been perfectly possible), and to sleep on. Up to now I've always been able to force myself not to do this; I realized that it would have been the first stage of capitulation, and that worse would probably have followed. An outward and purely physical régime (exercises and a cold wash down in the morning) itself provides some support for one's inner discipline. Further, there is nothing worse in such times than to try to find a substitute for the irreplaceable. It just does not work, and it leads to still greater indiscipline, for the strength to overcome tension (such strength can come only from looking the longing straight in the face) is impaired, and endurance becomes even more unbearable...

Another point: I don't think it is good to talk to strangers about our position; that always makes it even worse – although we ought to be ready, when occasion arises, to listen to other people. Above all, we must never give way to self-pity. And on the Christian aspect of the matter, there are some lines that say

> ... that we remember what we would forget,
> that this poor earth is not our home.

That is indeed something essential, but it must come last of all. I believe that we ought so to love and trust God in our *lives*, and in all the good things that he sends us, that when the time comes (but not before!) we may go to him with love, trust, and joy. But, to put it plainly, for a man in his wife's arms to be hankering after the other world is, in mild terms, a piece of bad taste, and not God's will. We ought to find and love God in what he actually gives us; if it pleases him to allow us to enjoy some overwhelming earthly happiness, we mustn't try to be more pious than God himself and allow our happiness to be corrupted by presumption and arrogance, and by unbridled religious fantasy which is never satisfied with what God gives. God will see to it that the man who finds him in his earthly happiness and thanks him for it does not lack reminder that earthly things are transient, that it is good for him to attune his heart to what is eternal, and that sooner or later there will be times when he can say in all sincerity, 'I wish I were home.' But everything has its time, and the main thing is that we keep step with God, and do not keep pressing on a few steps ahead – nor keep dawdling a step behind. It's presumptuous to want to have everything at once – matrimonial bliss, the cross, and the heavenly Jerusalem, where they neither marry nor are given in marriage. 'For everything there is a season' (Eccles. 3.1); everything has its time: 'a time to weep, and a time to laugh; ... a time to embrace, and a time to refrain from embracing; ... a time to rend, and a time to sew; ... and God seeks again what is past.' I suspect that these last words mean that nothing that is past is lost, that God gathers up again with us our past – and this may happen when we least expect it – we may be sure that it is only one of the many 'hours' that God is always holding ready for us. So we oughtn't to seek the past again by our own efforts, but only with God. Well, enough of this; I can see that I have taken on too much, for really in these matters I can tell you nothing that you don't know already.

Advent IV

What I wrote yesterday wasn't a Christmas letter. Today I must tell you above all how tremendously glad I am that you can spend Christmas at home. That's a piece of good fortune that no one has as easily as you!

The thought that you're celebrating the fifth Christmas of the war in freedom and with Renate is so comforting, and makes me so confident for the future, that I delight in it every day. You will celebrate a very splendid and joyful feast; and after what has happened to you so far, I don't think that it will be very long before you're on leave again in Berlin. And we'll celebrate Easter again in peace, won't we?

For this last week or so these lines have kept on running through my head:

> Let pass, dear brothers, every pain;
> What you have missed I'll bring again.

What does this 'I'll bring again' mean? It means that nothing is lost, that everything is taken up in Christ, although it is transformed, made transparent, clear, and free from all selfish desire. Christ restores all this as God originally intended it to be, without the distortion resulting from our sins. The doctrine derived from Eph. 1.10 – that of the restoration of all things, *anakephalaiosis*, *recapitulatio* (Irenaeus) – is a magnificent conception, full of comfort. This is how the promise 'God seeks what has been driven away' is fulfilled. And no one has expressed this so simply and artlessly as Paul Gerhardt in these words that he puts into the mouth of the Christ-child: 'I'll bring again'. Perhaps this line will help you a little in the coming weeks. Besides that, I've lately learnt for the first time to appreciate the hymn 'Beside thy cradle here I stand'. Up to now I hadn't made much of it; I suppose one has to be alone for a long time, and meditate on it, to be able to take it in properly. Every word is remarkably full of meaning and beauty. There's just a slight flavour of the monastery and mysticism, but no more than is justified. After all, it's right to speak of 'I' and 'Christ' as well as of 'we', and what that means can hardly be expressed better than it is in this hymn. There are also a few passages in a similar vein in the *Imitation of Christ*, which I'm reading now and then in the Latin (it reads much better in Latin than in German); and I sometimes think of

from the Augustinian *O bone Jesu* by Schütz. Doesn't this passage, in its ecstatic longing combined with pure devotion, suggest the 'bringing again' of all earthly desire? 'Bringing again' mustn't, of course, be confused with 'sublimation'; 'sublimation' is *sarx*, 'flesh' (and pietistic?), and 'restoration' is spirit, not in the sense of 'spiritualization' (which is also *sarx*), but of *kaine ktisis* through the *pneuma hagion*, a new creation through the Holy Spirit. I think this point is also very important when we have to talk to people who ask us about their relation to their dead. *'I will bring again'* – that is, we cannot and should not take it back ourselves, but allow Christ to give it back to us. (By the way, if I'm buried, I should like the choir to sing 'One thing I desire of the Lord', 'Hasten, God, to deliver me', and *O bone Jesu*.)

At midday on Christmas Eve a touching old wind-player is coming here at his own suggestion to perform some Christmas carols. But some people with good judgment think it only gives the prisoners the screaming miseries, and so makes the day even harder for them; one said that the effect is 'demoralizing', and I can well imagine it. In former years the prisoners are said to have whistled and kicked up a row, no doubt to stop themselves from becoming sentimental. I think, too, that in view of all the misery that prevails here, anything like a pretty-pretty, sentimental reminder of Christmas is out of place. A good personal message, a sermon, would be better; without something of the kind, music by itself may be positively dangerous. Please don't think that I'm in any way frightened of that for myself; I'm not, but I'm sorry for all those helpless young soldiers in their cells.

One will probably never quite get rid of the accumulated weight of all the oppressive experiences that come day after day, and I suppose it's right that this should be so. I'm thinking a great deal about a radical reform of the penal system, and I hope my ideas may be turned to account some day.

If this letter reaches you in time, please try to get me something good to read over Christmas. I asked for a few books some time ago, but they may not have been available. Something exciting would do quite well. And if you can get without difficulty Barth's *Doctrine of Predestination* (in sheets), or his *Doctrine of God*, please have them sent to me. *Please* don't come yourself unless you have permission to visit. Your time now is short, and belongs to Renate.

Today I read the account of the travels in Palestine which old

Soden did with Knopf; nothing special, but I conceived a plan to travel there with you after the war. It seems that one only gets something out of it as a theologian; for the laity too much of it is a disappointment. We'll take our wives to Italy and leave them there to wait for us. What do you think?

The propagandist with whom I walk every day is really getting more and more difficult to put up with. Whereas most people here do try to keep control of themselves, even in the most difficult cases, he has completely gone to pieces, and cuts a really sorry figure. I try to be as nice as I can to him, and talk to him as if he were a child. Sometimes it's almost comical. What is pleasanter is to hear that when I'm in the sick-bay in the afternoon the word goes round the kitchen or the garden, and the prisoners come up on some pretext or other because, they say, it's so nice to have a chat with me. Of course, that isn't really allowed, but I was pleased to hear about it, and I'm sure you will be too. But mind you don't let it get around...

22 December 1943

They seem to have made up their minds that I cannot be with you for Christmas, though no one ventures to tell me so. I wonder why; do they think I'm so easily upset? Or do they think it kinder to lull me from day to day with empty hopes?... The English have a very suitable word for this sort of thing – 'tantalizing'. Out of pure sympathy they've been 'tantalizing' Maria and me for a couple of weeks. If you had been there, Eberhard, you would have ... done the duty of a friend by telling me the truth. Tomorrow or the day after I should be able to talk to you ... That's an event. I must spare my parents and also Maria, but you I will not deceive in any way, nor must you deceive me. We haven't done that before, and mustn't do it ever. I won't be able to write to you again after our meeting. But I want to thank you now, today, for coming and for being there for me. If you write to Renate from Italy and can occasionally include a note for me, even if it's only a few words, you will make me very happy. Aren't there things like purification plants in lakes? You know my technical naïvete – but there is something like that, and that's what you are to me. I do want to convey to you somehow tomorrow that my attitude towards my case is unquestionably one of faith, and I feel that it has become too

49

much a matter of calculation and foresight. I'm not so much concerned about the rather artless question whether I shall be home for Christmas or not; I think I could willingly renounce that, if I could do so 'in faith', knowing that it was inevitable. I can (I hope) bear all things 'in faith', even my condemnation, and even the other consequences that I fear (Ps. 18.29), but to be anxiously looking ahead wears one down. Don't worry about me if something worse happens. Others of the brethren have already been through that. But faithless vacillation, endless deliberation without action, refusal to take any risks – that's a real danger. I must be able to know for certain that I am in God's hands, not in men's. Then everything becomes easy, even the severest privation. Now it's not a matter (I think I can say this truthfully) of my being 'undeservedly impatient', as people are probably saying, but of my facing everything in faith. In this regard, enemies are often much less dangerous than good friends. And I feel that you're the only one who understands that. I think that Maria, too, already feels rather the same thing. If you think of me, in the next days and weeks, please do so in this way (Ps. 60.12). And if you've something to say to me about it, be so good as to write it to me. I don't want to go through this affair without faith.

My own view is that I shall be released, or called up into the army, in January or February. If you can do anything – and want to – where you are about my joining you, don't let yourself be dissuaded by the suggestions of others. The only question is whether you have anyone there to whom you can speak in confidence. However, it would have to happen soon. We must learn to act differently from those who always hesitate, whose failure we know in a wider context. We must be clear about what we want, we must ask whether we're up to it, and then we must do it with unshakable confidence. Then and only then can we also bear the consequences.

Now I want to assure you that I haven't for a moment regretted coming back in 1939 – nor any of the consequences, either. I knew quite well what I was doing, and I acted with a clear conscience. I've no wish to cross out of my life anything that has happened since, either to me personally (would I have got engaged otherwise? would you have married? Sigurdshof, East Prussia, Ettal, my illness and all the help you gave me then, and the time in

50

Berlin), or as regards events in general. And I regard my being kept here (do you remember that I prophesied to you last March about what the year would bring?) as being involved in Germany's fate, as I was resolved to be. I don't look back on the past and accept the present reproachfully, but I don't want the machinations of men to make me waver. All we can do is to live in assurance and faith – you out there with the soldiers, and I in my cell. – I've just come across this in the *Imitation of Christ*: *Custodi diligenter cellam tuam, et custodiet te* ('Take good care of your cell, and it will take care of you'). – May God keep us in faith.

To Renate and Eberhard Bethge   Christmas Eve 1943

It's half past nine in the evening; I've been spending a few lovely peaceful hours, and thinking very gratefully about your being able to spend the day together ...

One of my greatest joys this Christmas is that we have again been able to exchange the Bible readings for the coming year. I had already thought of it and hoped for it, though I hardly expected that it would be possible. And now this book, which has meant so much to me in the past months, will be with us throughout next year too, and when we read it in the morning we shall think especially of each other. Many, many thanks. It was a particularly nice idea of yours to look for the beautiful book of poetry; I keep reading it and find much joy and gain in it. I was at first rather sad that I can't give you anything nice this time; but my thoughts and wishes have been closer than ever to you, if that is possible.

I should like to say something to help you in the time of separation that lies ahead. There is no need to say how hard any such separation is for us; but as I've now been separated for nine months from all the people that I'm devoted to, I have some experiences that I should like to pass on to you. So far, Eberhard and I have exchanged all the experiences that have been important to us, and this has been a great help to us; now you, Renate, will have some part in this. You must try to forget your 'uncle' and think more of your husband's friend.

First: nothing can make up for the absence of someone whom we love, and it would be wrong to try to find a substitute: we must simply hold out and see it through. That sounds very hard at first,

51

but at the same time it is a great consolation, for the gap, as long as it remains unfilled, preserves the bonds between us. It is nonsense to say that God fills the gap; he doesn't fill it, but on the contrary, he keeps it empty and so helps us to maintain our former communion with each other even at the cost of pain.

Secondly: the dearer and richer our memories, the more difficult the separation. But gratitude changes the pangs of memory into a tranquil joy. The beauties of the past are borne, not as a thorn in the flesh, but as a precious gift in themselves. We must take care not to wallow in our memories or hand ourselves over to them, just as we do not gaze all the time at a valuable present, but only at special times, and apart from these keep it simply as a hidden treasure that is ours for certain. In this way the past gives us lasting joy and strength.

Thirdly: times of separation are not a total loss or unprofitable for our companionship, or at any rate they need not be so. In spite of all the difficulties that they bring, they can be the means of strengthening fellowship quite remarkably.

Fourthly: I've learnt here especially that the *facts* can always be mastered, and that difficulties are magnified out of all proportion simply by fear and anxiety. From the moment we wake until we fall asleep we must commend other people wholly and unreservedly to God and leave them in his hands, and transform our anxiety for them into prayers on their behalf:

> With sorrow and with grief ...
> God *will not* be distracted.

Christmas Day

... Once more all my beautiful presents are arranged on the edge of my tipped-up bed, and in front of me are the pictures that I enjoy so much. I'm still relishing, almost uninterruptedly, the memory of your visit ... It really was a *necessitas*. The mind's hunger for discussion is much more tormenting than the body's hunger for food, and there is no one but you with whom I can talk about some things and in one way. A few pregnant remarks are enough to touch on a wide range of questions and clear them up. This ability to keep on the same wavelength, to play to each other, took years to cultivate, not always without friction, and we must never lose it.

52

It's an incredible gain, and extraordinarily helpful. What a great deal we touched on in that hour and a half, and how much we learnt from each other! Thank you very much for arranging the meeting successfully. It cost you and Renate a morning. But I think that nevertheless you were glad to do it. It *was* a *necessitas*, and now I can think of you again quite differently. By the way, your visit prompted me to a little work that perhaps I shall send you soon, and it has given me new courage and pleasure for the great work ...

The people here did their best to give me a happy Christmas, but I was glad to be alone again; I was surprised at that, and I sometimes wonder how I shall adapt myself to company again after this. You know how I used occasionally to retire to my own room after some great celebration. I'm afraid I must have grown even worse, for in spite of all my privations I've come to love solitude. I very much like to talk with two or three people, but I detest anything like a large assembly, and above all any chatter or gossip. Maria won't have an easy time with me in that respect.

To his parents   25 December 1943

Christmas is over. It brought me a few quiet, peaceful hours, and it revived a good many past memories. My gratitude for the preservation of yourselves and all the family in the heavy air raids, and my confidence that I shall see you again in the not too distant future, were greater than all my troubles. I lit the candles that you and Maria sent me, read the Christmas story and a few carols which I hummed over to myself; and in doing so, I thought of you all and hoped that, after all the alarms of the last few weeks, you might be able to enjoy an hour or two of peace. Your Christmas parcel was a great delight, especially great-grandfather's goblet from 1845, which is now standing on my table with evergreen in it. But the things to eat were also very fine, and will last for a while. I got interesting books and Christmas sweetmeats from the family; do thank them all very much. Maria, who was here on the 22nd, gave me the wrist-watch that her father was wearing when he was killed. That pleased me very much. She had also left a parcel for me, which was handed over early yesterday, packed in a most attractive way, with gingerbread, and greetings from her mother and grandmother. I felt rather sad that I wasn't able to give her anything; but I only want to do that when I'm free again and can give it to her myself; I told her this, and she also thought it was better that way. I'm quite sure that she will take these days of Christmas, in which she misses her father and brother and knows that I am in prison, as calmly and as bravely as she has endured everything else so far – even if it seems to be going beyond her strength. She has learnt very early to recognize a stronger and more gracious hand in what men inflict on us...

To his parents   14 January 1944

... I'm sitting by the open window, with the sunshine streaming in almost like spring, and I take this uncommonly fine start to the year for a good omen. Compared with last year, this year can only be better. – I'm getting on all right. I'm finding it a little easier to concentrate, and I'm enjoying Dilthey very much. I hope that I shall soon hear that you're on your way.

To Eberhard Bethge   [no date; sent on 18 January 1944]

... For some time I've been writing away at the small literary work that was prompted by our short meeting. But, as almost always, it's taking me more time than I expected at the beginning. I'll send it to you as soon as it's finished – if it's at all reasonable. In a rather haphazard way I've recently been reading a history of Scotland Yard, a history of prostitution, finished the Delbrück – I find him really rather uninteresting in his problems –, Reinhold Schneider's sonnets – very variable in quality, some very good; on the whole all the newest productions seem to me to be lacking in the *hilaritas* – 'cheerfulness' – which is to be found in any really great and free intellectual achievement. One has always the impression of a somewhat tortured and strained manufacture instead of creativity in the open air. Do you see what I mean? At the moment I'm reading a gigantic English novel which goes from 1500 to today, by Hugh Walpole, written in 1909. Dilthey is also interesting me very much and for an hour each day I'm studying the manual for medical staff, for any eventuality...

Over the last three days I've been reading a French novel, *Mariages* – not bad, but remarkably frank ... I was strengthened in my conviction that the naturalistic, psychological novel is no longer adequate for us. But we would have to talk about that later...

To Renate and Eberhard Bethge   23 January 1944

Since the ninth, my thoughts about you have taken a new shape. The fact that shortly before your parting you read the text Isa. 42.16 together puts these thoughts in a special light; on that day, which I knew had special significance for you, I kept reading the passages with special attention and great gratitude. That Sunday was a wrench for me as well as for you, though in a different way. It's a strange feeling to see a man whose life has in one way or another been so intimately bound up with one's own for years going out to meet an unknown future about which one can do virtually nothing. I think this realization of one's own helplessness has two sides, as you, Renate, also say: it brings both anxiety and relief. As long as we ourselves are trying to help shape someone else's destiny, we are never quite free of the question whether what we're doing is really for the other person's benefit – at least in any matter of great importance. But when all possibility of co-operating in anything is suddenly cut off, then behind any anxiety about him there is the consciousness that his life has now been placed wholly in better and stronger hands. For you, and for us, the greatest task during the coming weeks, and perhaps months, may be to entrust each other to those hands. When I learnt yesterday, Eberhard, that you are now somewhere south of Rome, this task became much clearer to me. I am to suppress all the questions that I may keep wanting to ask myself in this connection. Whatever weaknesses, miscalculations, and guilt there is in what precedes the facts, God is in the facts themselves. If we survive during these coming weeks or months, we shall be able to see quite clearly that all has turned out for the best. The idea that we could have avoided many of life's difficulties if we had taken things more cautiously is too foolish to be entertained for a moment. As I look back on your past I am so convinced that what has happened hitherto has been right, that I feel that what is happening now must be right too. To renounce a full life and its real joys in order to avoid pain is neither Christian nor human...

The news of the Nettuno landing has just come. I wonder whether you are anywhere thereabouts. When things like this happen, I see that composure isn't part of my nature, but that I have to acquire it at the cost of repeated effort. In fact, natural composure is probably in most cases nothing but a euphemism for indifference and indolence, and to that extent it's not very estimable. I read in Lessing recently: 'I am too proud to consider myself unlucky. Just clench your teeth and let your skiff sail where the wind and waves take it. Enough that I do not intend to upset it myself.' Is this pride and teeth-clenching to be completely forbidden and alien to the Christian, and replaced, shall we say, by a soft composure that gives way prematurely? Is there not also a kind of composure which is quite different from a dull, stolid, rigid, life-less, and above all thoughtless submitting-to-something-I-can't-help? I believe we honour God more if we recognize and explore and love all the values in the life that he gives us and therefore feel deep and sincere grief when these values are impaired or lost (some people are fond of mocking this attitude as the weakness and sensitivity of bourgeois life), than if we are insensitive to the values of life and may therefore also be insensitive to pain. Job's words, 'The Lord gave etc...', include rather than exclude this, as can be seen clearly enough from his teeth-clenching speeches which were vindicated by God (42.7ff.) in face of the false, pre-mature, pious submission of his friends...

I very much agree with what you say in this connection about friendship which, in contrast to marriage and kinship, has no generally recognized rights, and therefore depends entirely on its own inherent quality. It is by no means easy to classify friendship sociologically. Perhaps it is to be regarded as a sub-heading of culture and education, brotherhood being a sub-heading of church and comradeship a sub-heading of work and politics. Marriage, work, state, and church all have their definite, divine mandate; but what about culture and education? I don't think they can just be classified under work, however tempting that might be in many ways.

They belong, not to the sphere of obedience, but to the broad area of freedom, which surrounds all three spheres of the divine mandates. The man who is ignorant of this area of freedom may be a good father, citizen, and worker, indeed even a Christian; but I doubt whether he is a complete man and therefore a Christian in the widest sense of the term. Our 'Protestant' (not Lutheran) Prussian world has been so dominated by the four mandates that the sphere of freedom has receded into the background. I wonder whether it is possible (it almost seems so today) to regain the idea of the church as providing an understanding of the area of freedom (art, education, friendship, play), so that Kierkegaard's 'aesthetic existence' would not be banished from the church's sphere, but would be re-established within it? I really think that is so, and it would mean that we should recover a link with the Middle Ages. Who is there, for instance, in our times, who can devote himself with an easy mind to music, friendship, games, or happiness? Surely not the 'ethical' man, but only the Christian. Just because friendship belongs to this sphere of freedom ('of the Christian man'?!), it must be confidently defended against all the dis-approving frowns of 'ethical' existences, though without claiming for it the *necessitas* of a divine decree, but only the *necessitas* of *freedom*. I believe that within the sphere of this freedom friendship is by far the rarest and most priceless element, for where else does it survive in this world of ours, dominated as it is by the *first three* mandates? It cannot be compared with the elements of the mandates, for in relation to them it is *sui generis*, but it belongs to them as the cornflower belongs to the cornfield.

As to what you said about 'Christ's anguish': it comes out only in *prayer* (as it does in the Psalms). (I have never been clear why the evangelists report this prayer, which no one can have heard. The suggestion that Jesus revealed it to the disciples during the forty days is an evasion of the difficulty. Have you any comment?)

Your reference to Socrates in connection with the theme of culture and death may be very valuable; I must think about it. The only thing I am really clear about in the whole problem is that a 'culture' that breaks down in the face of danger is no culture. Culture must be able to face danger and death – *impavidum feriunt ruinae:* 'the ruins will strike a fearless man' (Horace) – even if it cannot 'conquer' them; what does 'conquer' mean? By finding forgiveness in judgment, and joy in terror? But we must discuss this further...

Have you paid a visit to the 'Propaganda' in Rome? What have you seen? Reminiscences of 1936 are very alive again, but you would know much more from that time than I. If you see the Laocoon again, just notice whether you don't think that the father's head may have been the model for later representations of Christ. Last time I saw this classical man of sorrows it impressed me deeply and kept me thinking for a long time. How wonderful it would be if we could be there together. You needn't worry about me. All goes well and there are a couple of really *very* nice people here, whom you must get to know some time later. If only we had got there already...

I've had to take a new line with the companion of my daily walks. Although he has done his best to ingratiate himself with me, he let fall a remark about the Gert [Jewish] problem, etc., lately that has made me more off-handed and cool to him than I have ever been to anyone before; I've also arranged for him to be deprived promptly of all little comforts. Now he feels obliged to go round whimpering for a time, but it leaves me – I am surprised at myself, but interested too – absolutely cold. He really is a pitiful figure, but certainly not 'poor Lazarus'...

To Eberhard Bethge   29 and 30 January 1944

... When I think of you every morning and evening, I have to try very hard not to let all my thoughts dwell on the many cares and anxieties that beset you, instead of praying for you properly. In that connection I must talk to you some time about prayer in time of trouble; it's a difficult matter, and yet our misgivings about it may not be good. Psalm 50 says quite clearly, 'Call upon me in the day of trouble; I will deliver you, and you shall glorify me.' The whole history of the children of Israel consists of such cries of help. And I must say that the last two nights have made me face this problem again in a quite elementary way. While the bombs are falling like that all round the building, I cannot help thinking of God, his judgment, his hand stretched out and his anger not turned away (Isa. 5.25 and 9.11–10.4), and of my own unpreparedness. I feel how men can make vows, and then I think of you all and say, 'better me than one of them' – and that makes me realize how attached I am to you all. I won't say anything more about it – it will have to be by word of mouth; but when all is said and done, it's true that it needs trouble to shake us up and drive us to prayer, though I feel every time that it is something to be ashamed of, as indeed it is. That may be because I haven't so far felt able to say a Christian word to the others at such a moment. As we were again lying on the floor last night, and someone exclaimed 'O God, O God' (he is normally a very flippant type), I couldn't bring myself to offer him any Christian encouragement or comfort; all I did was to look at my watch and say, 'It won't last more than ten minutes now.' There was nothing premeditated about it; it came quite automatically, and perhaps I felt that it was wrong to force religion down his throat just then. (Incidentally, Jesus didn't try to convert the two thieves on the cross; one of them turned to him!)

I'm sorry to say that I suffered a severe loss the night before last. The man who was, to my mind, by far the most intelligent and attractive in the place was killed in the city by a direct hit. I should certainly have put him in touch with you later, and we already had plans for the future. We often had interesting talks, and the other day he brought me *Daumier und die Justiz*, which I still have. He was a really educated man of working-class origin, a philosopher, and father of three children. I was very much distressed by his death.

In the last few days I've again been busy on the little work that I mentioned to you before, about the meeting of two old friends after they have been separated for a long time during the war. I hope to be able to send it to you soon. You needn't worry – it will *not* be a *roman à clef*...

In earlier times, even one of the problems that we are now having to deal with would have been enough to take up all our time. Now we have to reduce to a common denominator war, marriage, church, profession, housing, the possible death of those nearest and dearest to us and, added to that, my present situation. No doubt most people would regard these simply as separate problems, but for the Christian and the 'cultured' man that is impossible; he cannot split up his life or dismember it, and the common denominator must be sought both in thought and in a personal and integrated attitude to life. The man who allows himself to be torn into fragments by events and by questions has not passed the test for the present and the future. In the story of young Witiko we read that he set out into the world *'Um das Ganze zu tun'* (to do the whole thing); here we have the *anthropos teleios* (*teleios* originally means 'whole' in the sense of 'complete' or 'perfect'); 'You, therefore, must be perfect (*teleios*), as your heavenly Father is perfect' (Matt. 5.48) – in contrast to the *aner dipsychos* ('a double-minded man') of James 1.8. Witiko 'does the whole thing' by trying to adapt himself to the realities of life, by always listening to the advice of experienced people – i.e. by showing that he himself is a member of the 'whole'. We can never achieve this 'wholeness' simply by ourselves, but only together with others...

I have just started to read Harnack's *History of the Prussian Academy*; it is very good. I'm sure he put his heart and soul into it, and he said more than once that he considered it his best book. – How are you? Do let me know. I'm still surprisingly well. I suppose it makes some difference to know that I mustn't be ill here in any circumstances. I always find enough strength and concentration for reading, but not always for writing and productive work, though now and again things go very well. How I shall get used to living in company again I don't yet know...

To Eberhard Bethge   1 February 1944

...You may know that the last few nights have been bad, especially the night of 30 January. Those who had been bombed out came to me the next morning for a bit of comfort. But I'm afraid I'm bad at comforting; I can listen all right, but I can hardly ever find anything to say. But perhaps the way one asks about some things and not about others helps to suggest what really matters; and it seems to me more important actually to experience someone's distress than to brush it aside and retouch it. I've no sympathy with some fake interpretations of distress, because instead of being a comfort, they are the exact opposite. So I don't try to interpret it, and I think that is a responsible way to begin, although it's only a beginning, and I very seldom get beyond it. I sometimes think that real comfort must break in just as unexpectedly as the distress. But I admit that that may be a subterfuge.

Something that repeatedly puzzles me as well as other people is how quickly we forget about our impressions of a night's bombing. Even a few minutes after the all clear, almost everything that we had just been thinking about seems to vanish into thin air. With Luther a flash of lightning was enough to change the course of his life for years to come. Where is this 'memory' today? Is not the loss of this 'moral memory' (a horrid expression) responsible for the ruin of all obligations, of love, marriage, friendship, and loyalty? Nothing sticks fast, nothing holds firm; everything is here today and gone tomorrow. But the good things of life – truth, justice, and beauty – all great accomplishments need time, constancy, and 'memory', or they degenerate. The man who feels neither responsibility towards the past nor desire to shape the future is one who 'forgets', and I don't know how one can really get at such a person and bring him to his senses. Every word, even if it impresses him for the moment, goes in at one ear and out at the other. What is to be done about him? It is a great problem of Christian ministry. You put it very well recently when you said that people feel so quickly and so 'shamelessly at home'; I'm going to crib that expression from you, and make good use of it...

By the way, do you notice that uneducated people find it very difficult to decide things *objectively*, and that they allow some more or less fortuitous minor circumstance to turn the scales? It seems to me quite remarkable. I suppose one first has to take pains to *learn* to distinguish between thinking personally and thinking objectively; and, in fact, many people never learn to do so (see our professional colleagues, etc.).

2 February

... How much longer I shall have to go on amusing myself in my present place of residence is still just as uncertain as it was eight weeks ago. I'm using every day to do as much reading and work as possible, for what will happen afterwards is anybody's guess. Unfortunately the one thing I can't do is to get hold of the right books, and that upsets all my plans. I really wanted to become thoroughly familiar with the nineteenth century in Germany. I'm now feeling particularly the need of a good working knowledge of Dilthey, but his books are evidently not available. It's a matter of great regret to me that I'm so ignorant of the natural sciences, but it's a gap that cannot be filled now.

My present companion, whom I have mentioned several times in my letters, gets more and more pitiable. He has two colleagues here, one of whom spends the whole day moaning, and the other literally fills his trousers whenever the alert goes, and last night even when the first warning was sounded! When he told me about it yesterday – still moaning – I laughed outright and told him off, whereupon he would have me know that one mustn't laugh at anyone in distress or condemn him. I felt that that was really going too far, and I told him in no uncertain terms what I thought of people who can be very hard on others and talk big about a dangerous life and so on, and then collapse under the slightest test of endurance. I told him that it was a downright disgrace, that I had no sympathy at all with anyone like that, that I would throw any such specimens out of the party for making it look ridiculous, and so on. He was very surprised, and I dare say he thinks me a very doubtful Christian. Anyhow, these gentlemen's behaviour is already becoming a byword here, and the result can't be exactly pleasant for them. I find all this uncommonly instructive, though it's one of the most nauseating things that I've seen here so far. I don't really think I find it easy to despise anyone in trouble, and I said so quite unmistakably, which may have made his hair stand on end; but I can only regard that as contemptible. There are 17 and 18-year-olds here in much more dangerous places during the raids who behave splendidly, while these ... (I almost used an army term that would have surprised you) go round whimpering. It really makes me sick. Well, everyone makes a fool of himself as best he can.

I hope you won't think I've joined the ranks of the toughs; there is little enough occasion for that here, in any case. But there is a kind of weakness that Christianity does not hold with, but which people insist on claiming as Christian, and then sling mud at it. So we must take care that the contours do not get blurred.

Yesterday Susi brought me the big volume on Magdeburg Cathedral. I'm quite thrilled by the sculptures, especially some of the wise virgins. The bliss on these very earthly, almost peasant-like faces is really delightful and moving. Of course, you will know them well.

Today on my birthday morning, nothing is more natural for me than to write to you, remembering that for eight years in succession we celebrated the day together. Work is being laid aside for a few hours – it may take no harm from that – and I'm expecting a visit from Maria or my parents, although it's not yet quite certain whether it will come off. Eight years ago we were sitting at the fireside together. You had given me as a present the D major violin concerto, and we listened to it together; then I had to tell you a little about Harnack and past times; for some reason or other you enjoyed that very much, and afterwards we decided definitely to go to Sweden. A year later you gave me the September Bible with a lovely inscription and your name at the top. There followed Schlönwitz and Sigurdshof, and we had the company of a good many people who are no longer among us. The singing at the door, the prayer at the service that you undertook that day, the Claudius hymn, for which I'm indebted to Gerhard – all those things are delightful recollections that are proof against the horrible atmosphere of this place. I hope confidently that we shall be together again for your next birthday, and perhaps – who knows? – even for Easter. Then we shall get back to what is really our life's work; we shall have ample work that we shall enjoy, and what we have experienced in the meantime will not have been in vain. We shall probably always be grateful to each other for having been able to go through this present time as we're now doing. I know you're thinking of me today, and if your thoughts include not only the past, but also the hope of a future lived with a common purpose, even though in changed circumstances, then indeed I'm very happy...

– When I was in the middle of this letter, I was called downstairs, where the first thing with which Maria greeted me was the happy news: 'Renate has a little boy, and his name is Dietrich!' Everything went well; it took an hour and a half, and mother acted as midwife, with Christel's help! What a surprise, and what a delight! I'm happier than I can tell you. And how happy you, of all people, will be. And everything went so quickly and smoothly! So now you have a son, and all your thoughts will turn towards the future, full of hope. What possibilities there may be in him!...

Rüdiger's disposition and sensitive conscience, father's humanity – really a great many good forces have gathered together there, and it won't be long before they gradually develop. And so now he is really to be called Dietrich; I don't know what to say to that; I hope I can promise you to be a good godfather and 'great-'uncle(!), and I should be insincere if I didn't say that I'm immensely pleased and proud that you've named your first-born after me. The fact that his birthday comes one day before mine means, no doubt, that he will keep his independence *vis-a-vis* his namesake-uncle, and will always be a little ahead of him. I'm particularly pleased that the two days are so close to each other, and when he hears later on where his uncle was when he was told his name, perhaps that may leave some impression on him too. Thank you both very much for deciding to do this, and I think the others will be pleased about it too.

5 February

Yesterday, when so many people were showing such kindly concern for me, I completely forgot my own birthday, as my delight over little Dietrich's birthday put it right out of my head. Even the heartening little nosegay of flowers that some of my fellow inmates here picked for me remained in my thoughts by your little boy's bed. The day couldn't possibly have brought me any greater joy. It wasn't till I was going to sleep that I realized that you've pushed our family on by one generation – 3 February has created great-grandparents, grandparents, great-uncles and great-aunts, and young uncles and aunts! That's a fine achievement of yours; you've promoted me to the third generation!...

To Eberhard Bethge   12 February 1944

... Are you having a taste of spring yet? Here the winter is just beginning. In my imagination I live a good deal in nature, in the glades near Friedrichsbrunn, or on the slopes from which one can look beyond Treseburg to the Brocken. I lie on my back in the grass, watch the clouds sailing in the breeze across the blue sky, and listen to the rustling of the woods. It's remarkable how greatly these memories of childhood affect one's whole outlook; it would seem to me impossible and unnatural for us to have lived either up in the mountains or by the sea. It is the hills of central Germany, the Harz, the Thuringian forest, the Weserberge, that to me represent nature, that belong to me and have fashioned me. Of course, there are also a conventional Harz and a hikers' Wesergebirge, just as there are a fashionable and a Nietzschian Engadine, a romantic Rhineland, a Berliners' Baltic, and the ideal-ized poverty and melancholy of a fisherman's cottage. So perhaps 'my' central hills are 'bourgeois' in the sense of what is natural, not too high, modest and self-sufficient(?), unphilosophical, satisfied with concrete realities, and above all 'not-given-to-self-advertise-ment'. It would be very tempting to pursue this sociological treat-ment of nature some day. By the way, in reading Stifter I can see the difference between simpleness and simplicity. Stifter displays, not simpleness, but (as the 'bourgeois' does) simplicity. 'Simple-ness' is, even in theology, more of an aesthetic idea (was Winckel-mann really right about the 'noble simpleness' of classical art? That definition certainly does not apply to the Laocoon; I think 'still greatness' is very good), whereas 'simplicity' is an ethical one. One can acquire 'simplicity', but 'simpleness' is innate. Education and culture may bring 'simplicity' – indeed, it ought to be one of their essential aims – but simpleness is a gift. The two things seem to me to be related in much the same way as 'purity' and 'moderation'. One can only *be* 'pure', in relation to one's origin or goal, i.e. in relation to baptism or to forgiveness at the Lord's Supper; like 'simpleness' it involves the idea of totality. If we have lost our purity – and we have all lost it – it can be given back to us in faith; but in ourselves, as living and developing persons, we can no longer be 'pure', but only 'moderate', and that is a possible and a necessary aim of education and culture.

How does the Italian landscape impress you? Is there any Italian school of landscape painters, anything comparable to Thoma, or even to Claude Lorrain, Ruysdael, or Turner? Or is nature there so completely absorbed into art that it cannot be looked at for its own sake? All the good pictures that I can think of just now are of city life; I can't remember any that are purely of landscape.

13 February

I often notice here, both in myself and in others, the difference between the need to be communicative, the wish for conversation, and the desire for confession. The need to be communicative may perhaps on occasion be quite attractive in women, but I find it most repugnant in men. There is quite indiscriminate gossip, in front of all comers, about one's own affairs, no matter whether they interest or concern other people or not – simply, in fact, because one just has to gossip. It's an almost physical urge, but if you manage to suppress it for a few hours, you're glad afterwards that you didn't let yourself go. It sometimes makes me ashamed here to see how people lower themselves in their need to gossip, how they talk incessantly about their own affairs to others who are hardly worth wasting their breath on and who hardly even listen; and the strange thing is that these people do not even feel that they have to speak the truth, but simply want to talk about themselves, whether they tell the truth or not. The wish for a good conversation, a meeting of minds, is quite another matter; but there are very few people here who can carry on a conversation that goes beyond their own personal concerns. Again, the desire for confession is something quite different. I think it's infrequent here, because people are not primarily concerned here, either subjectively or objectively, about 'sin'. You may perhaps have noticed that in the prayers that I sent you the request for forgiveness of sins doesn't occupy the central place; I should consider it a complete mistake, both from a pastoral and from a practical point of view, to proceed on 'methodist' lines here. We must talk about that some day.

To Eberhard Bethge   21 February 1944

... I wonder whether my excessive scrupulousness, about which you often used to shake your head in amusement (I'm thinking of our travels), is not a negative side of bourgeois existence – simply part of our lack of faith, a part that remains hidden in times of security, but comes out in times of insecurity in the form of 'dread' (I don't mean 'cowardice', which is something different: 'dread' can show itself in recklessness as well as in cowardice), dread of

66

straightforward, simple actions, dread of having to make necessary decisions. I've often wondered here where we are to draw the line between necessary resistance to 'fate', and equally necessary submission. Don Quixote is the symbol of resistance carried to the point of absurdity, even lunacy; and similarly Michael Kohlhaas, insisting on his rights, puts himself in the wrong ... in both cases resistance at last defeats its own object, and evaporates in theoretical fantasy. Sancho Panza is the type of complacent and artful accommodation to things as they are. I think we must rise to the great demands that are made on us personally, and yet at the same time fulfil the commonplace and necessary tasks of daily life. We must confront fate – to me the neuter gender of the word 'fate' (*Schicksal*) is significant – as resolutely as we submit to it at the right time. One can speak of 'guidance' only on the other side of the twofold process, with God meeting us no longer as 'Thou', but also 'disguised' in the 'It'; so in the last resort my question is how we are to find the 'Thou' in this 'It' (i.e. fate), or, in other words, how does 'fate' really become 'guidance'? It's therefore impossible to define the boundary between resistance and submission on abstract principles; but both of them must be there and both must be shown with determination. Faith demands this elasticity of behaviour. Only so can we stand our ground in each situation as it arises, and turn it to gain.

23 February

If you have the chance of going to Rome during Holy Week, I advise you to attend the afternoon service at St Peter's on Maundy Thursday (from about 2 to 6). That is really the Good Friday service, as the Roman Catholic Church anticipates its feasts from noon on the previous day. As far as I remember (though I'm not quite certain), there is also a big service on the Wednesday. On Maundy Thursday the twelve candles on the altar are put out as a symbol of the disciples' flight, till in the vast space there is only one candle left burning in the middle – Christ. After that comes the cleansing of the altar. At about 7 a.m. on the Saturday there is the blessing of the water (as far as I can remember, that is connected with the ordination of young priests). Then at 12 noon the Easter Alleluia is sung, the organ plays again, the bells peal, and the pictures are unveiled. This is the real celebration of Easter. Somewhere in Rome I also saw a Greek Orthodox service, which at the time – more than twenty years ago! – impressed me very much. The service on Easter Eve in the Lateran (it starts in the Baptistery) is also very famous. If you happen to be on Monte Pincio towards sunset and are near the Church of Trinità del Monte, do see whether the nuns are singing just then; I heard them once, and was very impressed; I believe it's even mentioned in Baedeker.

I wonder how far you are directly involved in the fighting where you are. I suppose it's mainly a question of air raids, as it is here. The intensification of the war in the air in about the last ten days, and especially the heavy attacks in daylight, make one wonder whether the English are probing our air power as a prelude to invasion and as a means of pinning down our land forces inside Germany.

The longer we are uprooted from our professional activities and our private lives, the more we feel how fragmentary our lives are, compared with those of our parents. The portraits of the great savants in Harnack's *History of the Academy* make me acutely aware of that, and almost sadden me a little. Where is there an intellectual life's work today? Where are the collecting, assimilating, and developing of material necessary for producing such a work? Where is there today the combination of fine *abandon* and large-scale planning that goes with such a life? I doubt whether anything of the kind still exists, even among technicians and scientists, the only people who are still free to work in their own way. The end of the eighteenth century saw the end of the 'polymath', and in the nineteenth century intensive education replaced extensive, so that towards the end of it the 'specialist' evolved; and by now everyone is just a technician, even in the arts – in music the standard is high, in painting and poetry extremely moderate. This means that our cultural life remains a torso. The important thing today is that we should be able to discern from the fragment of our life how the whole was arranged and planned, and what material it consists of. For really, there are some fragments that are only worth throwing into the dustbin (even a decent 'hell' is too good for them), and others whose importance lasts for centuries, because their completion can only be a matter for God, and so they are fragments that must be fragments – I'm thinking, e.g., of the *Art of Fugue*. If our life is but the remotest reflection of such a fragment, if we accumulate, at least for a short time, a wealth of themes and weld them into a harmony in which the great counterpoint is maintained from start to finish, so that at last, when it breaks off abruptly, we can sing no more than the chorale, 'I come before thy throne', we will not bemoan the fragmentariness of our life, but rather rejoice in it. I can never get away from Jeremiah 45. Do you still remember that Saturday evening in Finkenwalde when I expounded it? Here, too, is a necessary fragment of life – 'but I will give you your life as a prize of war'. . .

To Eberhard Bethge   1 March 1944

I've nothing special to write to you today, but I don't want you to feel lonely, nor to believe for a moment that you are in any way forgotten, that one has in any way become resigned to your absence in a distant country. I want to let you know that as far as possible I'm living in a daily spiritual exchange with you; I can't read a book or write a paragraph without talking to you about it or at least asking myself what you would say about it. In short, all this automatically takes the form of this letter, even if there is really nothing 'to report'. I.e. there is, of course, enough to report, but one doesn't know where to begin and so one puts it off to the great moment of reunion. What a day it will be when you see your son for the first time (according to Maria's mother, who visited me recently, he is also said to be a bit like me, – the general view is that he looks like *you*, and that he has a particularly nice and open face), when you see Renate again – and finally, I also imagine to myself that you also look forward to being with me again and to discussing all that we've been through and learnt during a whole year. For myself at any rate, that is one of the greatest hopes for the near future. I suppose you, too, can sometimes hardly imagine that such a day will ever come. It's difficult to believe that there is any chance of our overcoming all the obstacles in our way, but 'that which tarries is all the sweeter when it comes . . .', and I must say I am entering on this new month with great hopes, and I think you are doing the same. I'm redoubling my efforts to make the best use of the last part of my time here. Perhaps your experiences, too, will be of great value to you all your life. The constant danger to which nearly all of us are at present exposed in one way or another provides a wonderful incentive to use the present moment, 'making the most of the time'. I sometimes feel that I'm living, just as long as I have something great to work for. Do you know this feeling, too? or is it rather mad?...

The less reflective part of your nature makes you a member of the younger generation rather than of my own, and to this extent I can even feel as though I'm an 'uncle' towards you. What has impressed you among us older ones is, I suppose, above all the security which has come through reflection and has hardened in this way, a reflection which has not led to intellectualism and thus to disintegration and relativism, but has entered into one's whole attitude to life and not weakened, but strengthened, the impulses of life. Nevertheless, I regard 'you younger ones' as being more competent than we are. People say in America that the negroes survived because they had not forgotten how to laugh, whereas the Indians went under because they were too 'proud'. What I mean lies somewhere in this direction.

To Eberhard Bethge   9 March 1944

... I haven't yet answered your remarks about Michelangelo, Burckhardt, and *hilaritas*. I found them illuminating – at any rate, what you say about Burckhardt's theses. But surely *hilaritas* means not only serenity, in the classical sense of the word (Raphael and Mozart); Walther v.d. Vogelweide, the Knight of Bamberg, Luther, Lessing, Rubens, Hugo Wolf, Karl Barth – to mention only a few – also have a kind of *hilaritas*, which I might describe as confidence in their own work, boldness and defiance of the world and of popular opinion, a steadfast certainty that in their own work they are showing the world something *good* (even if the world doesn't like it), and a high-spirited self-confidence. I admit that Michelangelo, Rembrandt and, at a considerable remove, Kierkegaard and Nietzsche, are in quite a different category from those that I've mentioned. There is something less assertive, evident, and final in their works, less conviction, detachment, and humour. All the same, I think some of them are characterized by *hilaritas* in the sense that I've described, as a necessary attribute of greatness. Here is Burckhardt's limitation, probably a conscious one.

I've recently been studying the mature 'worldliness' of the thirteenth century, conditioned, not by the Renaissance, but by the Middle Ages, and presumably by the struggle between the *idea of the emperor* and the papacy. (Walther, the Nibelungen, Parsifal – what surprising tolerance of the Mohammedans in the figure of Parsifal's half-brother Feirefiz! – Naumburg and Magdeburg cathedrals.) This worldliness is not 'emancipated', but 'Christian', even if it is anti-clerical. Where did this 'worldliness', so essentially different from that of the Renaissance, stop? A trace of it seems to survive in Lessing – in contrast to the Western Enlightenment – and in a different way in Goethe, then later in Stifter and Mörike (to say nothing of Claudius and Gotthelf), but nowhere in Schiller and the Idealists. It would be very useful to draw up a good genealogy here; and that raises the question of the value of classical antiquity. Is this still a real problem and a source of power for us, or not? The modern treatment of it under the heading 'city-state man' is already out of date, and the classicists' treatment of it from the aesthetic point of view has only a limited appeal today, and is something of a museum piece. The fundamental concepts of humanism – humanity, tolerance, gentleness, and moderation – are already present in their finest form in Wolfram von Eschenbach and in the Knight of Bamberg, and they are more accessible to us here than in classical antiquity itself. How far, then, does 'education' still depend on classical antiquity? Is the Ranke-to-Delbrück interpretation of history as a *continuum* consisting of 'classical antiquity', 'the middle ages', and 'modern times' really valid, or isn't Spengler also right with his theory of cultural phases as self-contained cycles, even though he gives too biological a twist to historical events? The notion of the historical *continuum* goes back to Hegel, who sees the whole course of history as culminating in 'modern times' – i.e. in his own system of philosophy. That notion is therefore *idealistic* (in spite of Ranke's assertion that every moment of history is 'immediate to God'; that assertion *might* have supplied a corrective of the whole conception of the *continuum* of development, but it didn't do so). Spengler's 'morphology' is *biological*, and that gives it its limitations (what does he mean by the 'senescence' and 'decline' of a culture?). For the concept of education, this means that we can neither idealistically accept classical antiquity as *the* foundation, nor simply eliminate it, biologically and morphologically, from our pattern of education. Until we can see further into it, it will be as well to base our attitude to the past, and to classical antiquity in particular, not on a general concept of history, but solely on *facts* and *achievements*. Perhaps you will bring back from Italy something important in this direction. Personally, I'm afraid, I've always felt cool towards the Renaissance and classicism; they seem to me somehow alien, and I cannot make them my own. I wonder whether a knowledge of other countries and an intimate contact with them are not more important for education today than a knowledge of the classics. In either case, of course, there is the possibility of philistinism; but perhaps one of our tasks is to see that our contacts with other peoples and countries reach out beyond politics or commerce or snobbishness to something really educational. In that way we should be tapping a hitherto unused source for the fertilizing of our education, and at the same time carrying on an old European tradition.

The loudspeakers are just announcing the approach of strong contingents of aircraft. We could see a good deal of the last two daylight raids on Berlin; there were fairly large formations flying through a cloudless sky and leaving vapour trails behind them, and at times there was plenty of flak. The alert was on for two and a half hours yesterday, longer than at night. Today the sky is overcast. I'm very glad that Renate is in Sakrow; also thinking of you. The siren is just going, so I must break off and write more later.

It lasted two hours. 'Bombs were dropped in all parts of the city,' say the loudspeakers. In the months here I've been trying to observe how far people believe in anything 'supernatural'. Three ideas seem to be widespread, each being partly expressed in some superstitious practice: (1) Time after time one hears 'Keep your fingers crossed', some sort of power being associated with the accompanying thought: people do not want to feel alone in times of danger, but to be sure of some invisible presence. (2) 'Touch wood' is the exclamation every evening, when the question is discussed 'whether they will come tonight or not'; this seems to be a recollection of the wrath of God on the *hubris* of man, a metaphysical, and not merely a moral reason for humility. (3) 'If it's got your number on, you'll get it', and therefore everyone may as well stay where he is. On a Christian interpretation these three points might be regarded as a recollection of intercession and community; of God's wrath and grace, and of divine guidance. To the last-mentioned we might add another remark that is very often heard here: 'Who knows what good may come of it?' There doesn't seem to me to be any trace of a recollection of eschatology. I wonder whether you've noticed anything different. Do write and tell me your thoughts on all this.

This is my second Passiontide here. When people suggest in their letters ... that I'm 'suffering' here, I reject the thought. It seems to me a profanation. These things mustn't be dramatized. I doubt very much whether I'm 'suffering' any more than you, or most people, are suffering today. Of course, a great deal here is horrible, but where isn't it? Perhaps we've made too much of this question of suffering, and been too solemn about it. I've some-times been surprised that the Roman Catholics take so little notice of that kind of thing. Does that make them stronger than we are? Perhaps they know better from their own history what suffering and martyrdom really are, and are silent about petty inconveni-ences and obstacles. I believe, for instance, that physical suffer-ings, actual pain and so on, are certainly to be classed as 'suffer-ing'. We so like to stress spiritual suffering; and yet that is just what Christ is supposed to have taken from us, and I can find nothing about it in the New Testament, or in the acts of the early martyrs. After all, whether 'the church suffers' is not at all the same as whether one of its servants has to put up with this or that. I think we need a good deal of correction on this point; indeed, I must admit candidly that I sometimes feel almost ashamed of how often we've talked about our own sufferings. No, suffering must be something quite different, and have a quite different dimension, from what I've so far experienced...

To Eberhard Bethge   Laetare [19 March 1944]

With the news of the heavy fighting in your neighbourhood, you're hardly ever out of my thoughts; every word that I read in the Bible, and every line of a hymn, I apply to you. You must be feeling particularly homesick ... in these dangerous days, and every letter will only make it worse. But isn't it characteristic of a man, in contrast to an immature person, that his centre of gravity is always where he actually is, and that the longing for the fulfilment of his wishes cannot prevent him from being his whole self, wherever he happens to be? The adolescent is never wholly in one place; that is one of his essential characteristics, else he would presumably be a dullard. There is a wholeness about the fully grown man which enables him to face an existing situation squarely. He may have his longings, but he keeps them out of sight, and somehow masters them; and the more he has to over-come in order to live fully in the present, the more he will have the respect and confidence of his fellows, especially the younger ones, who are still on the road that he has already travelled. Desires to which we cling closely can easily prevent us from being what we ought to be and can be; and on the other hand, desires repeatedly mastered for the sake of present duty make us richer. Lack of desire is poverty. Almost all the people that I find in my present surroundings cling to their own desires, and so have no interest in others; they no longer listen, and they're incapable of loving their neighbour. I think that even in this place we ought to live as if we had no wishes and no future, and just be our true selves. It's remarkable then how others come to rely on us, confide in us, and let us talk to them. I'm writing all this to you because I think you have a big task on hand just now, and because you will be glad to think, later on, that you carried it out as well as you could. When we know that someone is in danger, we want to be sure that we know him as he really is. We can have abundant life, even though many wishes remain unfulfilled – that's what I have really been trying to say. Forgive me for putting such 'considerations' before you so persistently, but I'm sure you will understand that con-sidering things takes up a large part of my life here. For the rest, I must add, as a necessary supplement to what I've just written, that I'm more convinced than ever that our wishes are going to be fulfilled, and that there is no need for us to throw up the sponge. . .

Once again I'm having weeks when I don't read the Bible much; I never know quite what to do about it. I have no feeling of obligation about it, and I know, too, that after some time I shall plunge into it again voraciously. May one accept this as an entirely 'natural' mental process? I'm almost inclined to think so; it also happened, you know, during our *vita communis*. Of course, there's always the danger of laziness, but it would be wrong to get anxious about it; we can depend upon it that after the compass has wobbled a bit, it will point in the right direction again. Don't you agree? Did that reading Genesis 41.52 recently do you as much good as it did me? I hadn't come across it before. It's now a year since we spent those last days and did those last things together, and since I was able to be witness at your engagement. I keep being amazed that I was able to be with you on that day ... I'm curious as to how the future will lead us on, whether perhaps we shall be together again in our work – which I should very much like, or whether we shall have to be content with what has been. They really were quite wonderful years...

To Eberhard Bethge 24 March 1944

... I expect the question of your child's baptism is on your mind a good deal now, and that's mainly why I am writing to you, as I think you may be troubled by a certain 'inconsistency' about it. We've sometimes urged that children should be baptized as soon as possible (as it is a question of a sacrament), even if the father cannot be present. The reasons are clear. Yet I'm bound to agree that you will do well to wait. Why? I still think it is right and desirable (especially as an example to the community, and in particular for a pastor) to have one's child baptized soon, assuming that it is done with a sincere faith in the efficacy of the sacrament. At the same time, the father's wish to be present and to take part in the action with prayers for his child has relative justification. And when I examine myself, I must admit that I'm chiefly influenced by the thought that God also loves the still unbaptized child who is to be baptized later. The New Testament lays down no law about infant baptism; it is a gift of grace bestowed on the church, a gift that may be received and used in firm faith, and can thus be a striking testimony of faith for the community; but to force oneself to it without the compulsion of faith is not biblical. Infant baptism loses its justification only as a demonstration. God will not fail to hear prayers for a child and for a speedy coming of the day when we can bring him to the font together. As long as there is a justifiable hope that that day is not far off, I cannot believe that God is concerned about the exact date. So we can quite well wait a little and trust in God's kindly providence, and do later with a stronger faith what we should at the moment feel simply to be burdensome law ... So I should wait for a while (without any scruples!); we shall see our way more clearly later. I believe that the motivation behind the baptism and the way in which it can be performed most strongly in faith, may be more important than observing the letter of the law...

25 March

We had another very lively time last night. The view from the roof here over the city was staggering. I've heard nothing yet about the family. Thank God my parents went to Pätzig yesterday; but there wasn't much doing in the West. It seems to me absurd how one can't help hoping, when an air raid is announced, that it will be the turn of other places this time – as the saying goes, 'Holy St Florian, spare my house, set others on fire' – wanting to push off on to others what one fears for oneself: 'Perhaps they will get no further than Magdeburg or Stettin this time'; how often I've heard that fervent wish expressed! Such moments make one very conscious of *natura corrupta* and *peccatum originale*, and to that extent they may be quite salutary. Incidentally, there has been a very marked increase in air activity during the last few days, and it makes one wonder whether it isn't a substitute for the invasion that isn't materializing...

You're quite right about the rarity of landscape painting in the South generally. Is the south of France an exception – and Gauguin? or perhaps they weren't southerners? I don't know. What about Claude Lorrain? Yet it's alive in Germany and England. The southerner *has* the beauty of nature, while we long for it and love it wistfully, as a rarity. By the way, to change the subject: Mörike once said that 'where beauty is, there is happiness too'. Doesn't that fit in with Burckhardt? We're apt to acquiesce in Nietzsche's crude alternatives, as if the only concepts of beauty were on the one hand the 'Apolline' and on the other the 'Dionysian', or, as we should now say, the demonic. That's not so at all. Take, for example, Brueghel or Velasquez, or even Hans Thoma, Leopold von Kalckreuth, or the French impressionists. There we have a

76

beauty that is neither classical nor demonic, but simply earthly, and has a justification all of its own. For myself, I must say that it's the only kind of beauty that really appeals to me. I would include the Magdeburg virgins I mentioned and the Naumburg sculptures. May not the 'Faustian' interpretation of Gothic art be on altogether wrong lines? How else would there be such a contrast between the plastic arts and architecture?...

That must be all for today, or you would never get through this letter. I'm so glad to remember how you played the cantata 'Praise the Lord' that time. It did us all a lot of good!

27 March

Perhaps I already ought to be sending you my special good wishes for Easter, as I don't know how long it takes for letters to reach you and I would very much like you to know that in the weeks before and after Easter I know that I'm one with you in many good memories. In looking through *Das Neue Lied* these days, I'm constantly reminded that it is mainly to you that I owe my enjoyment of the Easter hymns. It's a year now since I heard a hymn sung. But it's strange how the music that we hear inwardly can almost surpass, if we really concentrate on it, what we hear physically. It has a greater purity, the dross falls away, and in a way the music acquires a 'new body'. There are only a few pieces that I know well enough to be able to hear them inwardly, but I manage this particularly well with the Easter hymns. I'm getting a better existential appreciation of the music that Beethoven composed after he had gone deaf, in particular the great set of variations from Opus 111, which we once heard together played by Gieseking:

By the way, I've sometimes listened lately to the Sunday evening concert from 6 to 7, though reception is atrocious...

Easter? We're paying more attention to dying than to death. We're more concerned to get over the act of dying than to overcome death. Socrates mastered the art of dying; Christ overcame death as 'the last enemy' (I Cor. 15.26). There is a real difference between the two things; the one is within the scope of human possibilities, the other means resurrection. It's not from *ars moriendi*, the art of dying, but from the resurrection of Christ, that a new and purifying wind can blow through our present world. *Here* is the answer to *dos moi pou sto kai kineso ten gen* [Give me somewhere to stand and I will move the world]. If a few people really believed that and acted on it in their daily lives, a great deal would be changed. To live in the light of the resurrection – that is what Easter means. Do you find, too, that most people don't know what they really live by? This *perturbatio animorum* spreads amazingly. It's an unconscious waiting for the word of deliverance, though the time is probably not yet ripe for it to be heard. But the time will come, and this Easter may be one of our last chances to prepare ourselves for our great task of the future. I hope you will be able to enjoy it, in spite of all the hardships that you're having to bear.

To Eberhard Bethge   2 April 1944

... Just fancy, I've suddenly, by an odd chance, taken up graphology again, and am enjoying it very much; I'm now working through Ludwig Klages' book. But I'm not going to try it on my friends and relatives; there are enough people here who are interested in it. I'm convinced of the thing's reliability. I expect you know that I was so successful at it as a young student that it became uncomfortable and I gave it up. That was almost 20 years ago. Now, having, I think, got over the dangers of psychology, I'm very interested in it again, and I should like to discuss it with you. If it gets uncanny again, I shall drop it at once. I think it possible that you might be very successful at it, as it needs two things, the second of which you have in much greater measure than I: sensitivity, and an acute power of observation. If you like, I will write to you again about it.

In the 800-page biography of Klopstock by Karl Kindt (formerly G[erman] Christian), 1941, I found some very striking extracts from Klopstock's play *Der Tod Adams*, which is about the death of the first man. The idea is interesting enough, and the play itself is powerful. I had sometimes thought of trying to rehabilitate Klopstock, so the book interests me very much.

Maria's birthday is on 23 April. Will you perhaps send her a brief greeting? She would certainly like it very much ... Well, that was simply a narrative letter which arose solely from a desire to talk to you this morning (in other times we would have made glorious music today) and not to leave you without news.

I have here a very detailed map of the environs of Rome; I often look at it when I'm thinking of you, and imagine you going round the streets with which you are familiar from long acquaintance hearing the sounds of war not very far away, and looking at the lake from the mountains.

Report on Prison Life after One Year in Tegel

The formalities of admission were correctly completed. For the first night I was locked up in an admission cell. The blankets on the camp bed had such a foul smell that in spite of the cold it was impossible to use them. Next morning a piece of bread was thrown into my cell; I had to pick it up from the floor. A quarter of the coffee consisted of grounds. The sound of the prison staff's vile abuse of the prisoners who were held for investigation penetrated into my cell for the first time; since then I have heard it every day from morning till night. When I had to parade with the other new arrivals, we were addressed by one of the jailers as 'blackguards', etc. etc. We were asked why we had been arrested, and when I said I did not know, the jailer answered with a scornful laugh, 'You'll find that out soon enough.' It was six months before I got a warrant for my arrest. As we went through the various offices, some NCOs, who had heard what my profession was, wanted now and then to have a few words with me. They were told that no one was to talk to me. While I was having a bath an NCO (I do not know who he was) suddenly appeared and asked me whether I knew Pastor N. [Martin Niemöller]. When I said that I did, he exclaimed, 'He is a good friend of mine,' and disappeared again. I was taken to the most isolated single cell on the top floor; a notice, prohibiting all access without special permission, was put outside it. I was told that all my correspondence would be stopped until further notice, and that, unlike all the other prisoners, I should not be allowed half an hour a day in the open air, although, according to the prison rules, I was entitled to it. I received neither newspapers nor anything to smoke. After 48 hours my Bible was returned to me; it had been searched to see whether I had smuggled inside it a saw, razor, or the like. For the next twelve days the cell door was opened only for bringing food in and putting the bucket out. No one said a word to me. I was told nothing about the reason for my detention, or how long it would last. I gathered from various remarks – and it was confirmed later – that I was lodged in the section for the most serious cases, where the condemned prisoners lay shackled.

The first night in my cell I could not sleep much, because in the next cell a prisoner wept loudly for several hours on end; no one took any notice. I thought at the time that that kind of thing would happen every night, but in all the months since then it has only been repeated once. In those first days of complete isolation I could see nothing of how things were run in the building; I could only picture what was going on from the incessant shouting of the warders. My basic impression, which is still unchanged, was that anyone detailed for investigation was at once treated as a criminal, and that in practice it was impossible for a prisoner who was treated unjustly to get redress. Later I more than once heard conversations in which warders said quite bluntly that if a prisoner complained of unjust treatment, or of being struck (which is strictly forbidden), the authorities would never believe the prisoner, but always the warder, especially as the latter could be sure of finding a colleague who would testify for him on oath. I have, in fact, known of cases where this evil practice was followed.

After twelve days the authorities got to know of my family connections. While this was a great relief to me personally, it was most embarrassing to see how everything changed from that moment. I was put into a more spacious cell, which one of the men cleaned every day for me; I was offered larger rations, which I always refused, as they would have been at the expense of the other prisoners; the captain fetched me for a daily walk, with the result that the staff treated me with studied politeness – in fact, several of them came to apologize: 'We didn't know', etc. It was painful.

General Treatment: The tone is set by those warders who behave in the most evil and brutal way towards the prisoners. The whole

80

building resounds with vile and insulting abuse, so that the quieter and more fair-minded warders, too, are nauseated by it, but they can hardly exercise any influence. During months of detention for investigation, prisoners who are later acquitted have to suffer abuse like criminals, and are absolutely defenceless, since their right to complain exists only in theory. Private means, cigarettes, and promises for later on play an important part. The little man with no connections, etc., has to submit to everything. The same people who rant and rage at the other prisoners show a servile politeness towards me. Attempts to have a quiet word with them about the treatment of all the other prisoners fail because, although they admit everything at the time, they are just as bad as ever an hour later. I must not omit to say that a number of the warders are even-tempered, matter-of-fact and, as far as possible, friendly towards the prisoners; but they mostly remain in subordinate posts.

Food: Prisoners cannot avoid the impression that they do not receive in full the rations due to them. There is often not the slightest trace of the meat that is alleged to be included in the soup. Bread and sausage are divided very unequally. I weighed one sausage ration myself; it was 15 grammes instead of 25. NCO's and others working in the kitchen have plenty of unhappy impressions and observations about this. With 700 prisoners to be fed, even the smallest inaccuracy makes a big difference. I know for a fact that when the doctors or officers inspect the prisoners' food, a nourishing sauce made of meat or cream is added to the plates concerned; and so it is not surprising that the prisoners' food has a high reputation. I also know that the meat intended for the prisoners has all the goodness boiled out of it first in the cauldrons where the staff's food is cooked, and so on. an occasional comparison between the prisoners' food and the staff's is simply staggering. On Sundays and holidays the food is not examined, and the mid-day meal is beneath all criticism; it consists of cabbage soup made with water and with no fat, meat, or potatoes at all. It seems to me beyond doubt that the food provided is quite inadequate for young people detained for any length of time. No records are kept of the prisoners' weight. Although these prisoners are only being held for investigation, and are, moreover, soldiers, some of whom are sent straight back to their untis when they are released, they are told that they are strictly forbidden, on pain of severe punishment, to receive food parcels. No articles of food are allowed in – not even the eggs and sandwiches that the prisoners' relatives bring them on visiting days. This causes great bitterness among the prisoners and their visitors. Military police who deliver the prisoners are looked after – against standing orders – in the kitchen.

Occupation; By far the greater part of the prisoners detained for investigation spend the day without any work, although most of them ask for work. They receive three books a week from a very mediocre library. Games of every kind, such as chess, are forbidden, even in the communal cells, and if any of the prisoners have managed to make themselves one, it is taken away from them and they are punished. There are no projects for work that would be useful for all the 700 prisoners, such as, for instance, the construction of air-raid shelters. There are no religious services. The prisoners, some of whom are very young (they include anti-aircraft auxiliaries), are bound to suffer in body and soul from the lack of occupation and of supervision, particularly during a long, solitary confinement.

Lighting; During the winter months the prisoners often had to sit in the dark for several hours because the staff were too lazy to switch on the cell lights. When the prisoners, who have a right to lighting in their cells, put out their flags or knocked to get attention, the staff would shout angrily at them, and the light would not be switched on till the next day. The prisoners are not allowed to lie on their beds before the Last Post so that they had to spend the hours before that sitting in the dark. That is very depressing, and only causes bitterness.

Air-raid warnings: There are no air-raid shelters for the prisoners. With all the labour available here, it would have been quite easy to provide these in good time. A command bunker has been built, but only for the governor's staff; otherwise, all that happens is that the prisoners on the top floor are locked in with the others in the ground-floor cells. When I asked why the prisoners in the second-floor cells were not moved down to the first floor, I was told that it would make too much work. There is no first-aid shelter. When the sick-bay was put out of action during a heavy attack, they could not start to bandage the injured till after it was over. No one who has experienced it will ever forget the shouting and screaming of the locked-up prisoners during a heavy air raid – some of them are here because of trifling offences, or are actually innocent. Seven hundred soldiers are exposed here to the dangers of a bombing attack with no protection.

Miscellaneous: The only way in which a prisoner can communicate with the staff in case of urgency is by putting out the flag. This is often ignored for hours, or perhaps a passing warder simply pushes it back without finding out what the prisoner wants. If the prisoner then knocks on the door, he gets a volley of abuse. If he reports sick outside the regulation hours, he inconveniences the staff, and is therefore in most cases angrily shouted at; it is only with great difficulty that he manages to gain access to the sick-bay. I have twice known prisoners to be kicked into it; one of them had acute appendicitis and had to be taken to the military hospital at once, and the other was suffering from prolonged hysterical convulsions. – All those who are detained for investigation, even for the most minor offences, appear in chains at their interrogation and trial. This is a great humiliation for a soldier in uniform, and makes the interrogation a more severe ordeal for him. – The men who empty the buckets and bring round the food receive the same amount of soap for washing as the ordinary prisoners, and even for the latter it is hardly enough.

To Eberhard Bethge   11 April 1944

I really intended to write to you at Easter, but I had so many well-meaning visitors that I had less peace and quiet then I should have liked. I didn't even manage to get a letter to Maria finished. I've got so used to the silence of solitude by now that after a short time I long for it again. I can't imagine myself spending the day as I used to, or even as you have to spend it now. You know that even earlier I couldn't take family festivals very well; I hope that this tendency hasn't grown too much now. I would certainly like to have a good talk with someone, but aimless gossip gets on my nerves terribly. The same is true of the usual music on the wireless; I just don't feel that it's music at all, but a quite empty racket.

There's surely a danger in all this. Nevertheless, I expect that you often feel the same way. Feelings of quality just cannot be killed, but grow stronger from year to year.

How did you spend Easter? Were you in Rome? How did you get over your homesickness? I should imagine that that is more difficult in your position than in mine, for it cannot be done merely through diversion and distraction. You need to get right down to fundamentals, to come to terms with life, and for that you need plenty of time to yourself. I find these first warm days of spring rather trying, and I expect you do too. When nature is rediscovering herself, and the actual communities in which we live remain in unresolved tension, we feel the discord particularly keenly. Or it may be really nothing but homesickness, which it's good for us to feel again keenly. At any rate, I must say that I myself have lived for many, many years quite absorbed in aims and tasks and hopes without any personal longings; and perhaps that has made me old before my time. It has made everything too 'matter-of-fact'. Almost everyone has aims and tasks, and everything is objectified, reified to such a tremendous extent – how many people today allow themselves any strong personal feeling and real yearning, or take the trouble to spend their strength freely in working out and carrying out that yearning, and letting it bear fruit? Those sentimental radio hits, with their artificial naïveté and empty crudities, are the pitiful remains and the maximum that people will tolerate by way of mental effort; it's a ghastly desolation and impoverishment. By contrast, we can be very glad when something affects us deeply, and regard the accompanying pains as an enrichment. High tensions produce big sparks (isn't that a physical fact? If it isn't, then translate it into the right kind of language). I've long had a special affection for the season between Easter and Ascension Day. Here's another great tension. How can people stand earthly tensions if they know nothing of the tension between heaven and earth? Have you by chance a copy of *Das Neue Lied* with you? I well remember learning the Ascension hymns with you, among them the one that I'm fondest of today: 'On this day we remember . . .' Just about now, by the way, we are beginning the tenth year of our friendship; that's a fairly large slice of one's life, and in the past year we've shared things together almost as closely as in the previous years of our *vita communis*. . ..

I heard someone say yesterday that the last years had been completely lost as far as he was concerned. I'm very glad that I have never yet had that feeling, even for a moment. Nor have I ever regretted my decision in the summer of 1939, for I'm firmly convinced – however strange it may seem – that my life has followed a straight and unbroken course, at any rate in its outward direction. It has been an uninterrupted enrichment of experience, for which I can only be thankful. If I were to end my life here in these conditions, that would have a meaning that I think I would understand; on the other hand, everything might be a thorough preparation for a new start, with marriage, peace, and new work...

Now I'm going to close for today; I must do another graphological analysis; that is the way in which I now spend the hours in which I cannot work properly. This letter is somewhat disjointed, as it was written with constant interruptions. Nevertheless, I expect that you will find it better than nothing. I often think of you each day and commend you to God.

To Eberhard Bethge   22 April 1944

... When you write that my time here will be very important for my professional work, and that you're very much looking forward to what I shall have to tell you later, and to what I've written, you mustn't indulge in any illusions about me. I've certainly learnt a great deal, but I don't think I have changed very much. There are people who change, and others who can hardly change at all. I don't think I've ever changed very much, except perhaps at the time of my first impressions abroad and under the first conscious influence of father's personality. It was then that I turned from phraseology to reality. I don't think, in fact, that you yourself have changed much. Self-development is, of course, a different matter. Neither of us has really had a break in our lives. Of course, we have deliberately broken with a good deal, but that again is something quite different. Even our present experiences probably don't represent a break in the passive sense. I sometimes used to long for something of the kind, but today I think differently about it. Continuity with one's own past is a great gift, too. Paul wrote II Tim.1.3a as well as I Tim.1.13. I'm often surprised how little (in contrast to nearly all the others here) I grub among my past mistakes and think how different one thing or another would be today if I had acted differently in the past; it doesn't worry me at all. Everything seems to have taken its natural course, and to be determined necessarily and straightforwardly by a higher providence. Do you feel the same?

I've often wondered lately why we grow insensitive to hardships in the course of time. When I think how I felt for weeks a year ago, it strikes me very much. I now see the same things quite differently. To put it down to nature's self-protection doesn't seem to me adequate; I'm more inclined to think that it may come from a clearer and more sober estimate of our own limitations and possibilities, which makes it possible for us genuinely to love our neighbour; as long as we let our imagination run riot, love of one's neighbour remains something vague and general. Today I can take a calmer view of other people, their predicaments and needs, and so I'm better able to serve them. I would speak of clarification rather than of insensitiveness; but of course, we are always having to try to change one into the other. I don't think we need reproach ourselves just because our feelings grow cooler and calmer in the course of time, though, of course, we must always be aware of the danger of not seeing the wood for the trees and keep alive strong feelings along with the clarification. Do these experiences mean anything to you, too?

I wonder why it is that we find some days so much more oppressive than others, for no apparent reason. Is it growing pains – or spiritual trial? Once they're over, the world looks quite a different place again.

The other day I heard the angel scene from *Palestrina* on the wireless, and thought of Munich. Even then, that was the only part that I specially liked. There is a great *Palestrina* fan here who cannot understand why I didn't specially care for it, and he was quite thrilled when I enjoyed the angel scene...

To his parents   26 April 1944

As it will presumably be a while after your last visit until I can talk to you, I would like to let you have at least a letter so that you know that things are well with me. This is my second spring in prison, but it's very different from last year's. Then all my impressions were fresh and vivid, and privations and pleasures were felt more keenly. Since then something has happened which I should never have thought possible – I've got used to things; and the only question is which has been greater, the growth of insensitivity or the clarification of experience – it probably varies in different connections. The things towards which we become insensitive are soon forgotten, as they're of no great consequence; but there are other things, which we have consciously or unconsciously assimilated and cannot forget. Intense experience forges them into convictions, resolutions, and plans, and as such they're important for our lives in the future. It certainly makes a great difference whether one is in prison for a month or a year; in the latter case one absorbs not only an interesting or intense impression, but a radically new kind of life. At the same time I think that certain inward preconditions are necessary to enable one to assimilate this particular aspect of life without danger, and I think a long imprisonment is extremely dangerous for very young people as far as their spiritual development is concerned. The impressions come with such violence that they may well sweep a great deal overboard.

I must thank you very much for the way you're continually making things easier for me by your regular visits, letters, and parcels. The great joy that your greetings give me has remained constant from the first, and always encourages me afresh to use my time here to the full. Thank you, too, for all the letters from the family – I had very nice letters again from Ursel and Karl-Friedrich. I wonder whether you could try to get me Ortega y Gasset's new book, *The Nature of Historical Crises*, and, if possible, his earlier work, *History as a System*; also H. Pfeffer, *The British Empire and the USA*?...

To Eberhard Bethge   30 April 1944

Another month gone. Does time fly as fast with you as it does with me here? I'm often surprised at it myself – and when will the month come when you and Renate, I and Maria, and we two are reunited? I have such a strong feeling that great events are moving the world every day and could change all our personal relationships, and I should like to write to you much oftener, partly

87

because I don't know how much longer I shall be able to, and even more because we want to share everything with each other as often and as long as we can. I'm firmly convinced that, by the time you get this letter, great decisions will already be setting things moving on all fronts. During the coming weeks we shall need great inner strength, and that is what I wish you. We shall have to keep all our wits about us, so as to let nothing scare us. In view of what is coming, I'm almost inclined to quote the biblical *dei* ['it must'], and I feel that I 'long to look', like the angels in I Peter 1.12, to see how God is going to solve the apparently insoluble. I think that God is now about to accomplish something that, whether we take part in it outwardly or inwardly, we can only receive with the greatest wonder and awe. Somehow it will be clear – for those who have eyes to see – that Ps. 58.11b and Ps. 9.19f. are true; and we shall have to repeat Jer. 45.4 to ourselves every day. It's harder for you to go through this separated from Renate and your child than it is for me, so I will think of you especially, as I am already doing now.

How good it would seem to me, for both of us, if we could go through this time together, helping each other. But it's probably 'better' for it not to be so, but for each of us to have to go through it alone. I find it hard not to be able to help you in anything – except by thinking of you every morning and evening when I read the Bible, and often during the day as well. You've no need to worry about me at all, as I'm getting on uncommonly well – you would be surprised, if you came to see me. People here keep on telling me (as you can see, I feel very flattered by it) that I'm 'radiating so much peace around me', and that I'm 'always so cheerful', – so that the feelings that I sometimes have to the contrary must, I suppose, rest on an illusion (not that I really believe that at all!). You would be surprised, and perhaps even worried, by my theological thoughts and the conclusions that they lead to; and this is where I miss you most of all, because I don't know anyone else with whom I could so well discuss them to have my thinking clarified.

What is bothering me incessantly is the question what Christianity really is, or indeed who Christ really is, for us today. The time when people could be told everything by means of words, whether theological or pious, is over, and so is the time of inwardness and conscience – and that means the time of religion in general. We are moving towards a completely religionless time; people as they are

88

now simply cannot be religious any more. Even those who honestly describe themselves as 'religious' do not in the least act up to it, and so they presumably mean something quite different by 'religious'.

Our whole nineteen-hundred-year-old Christian proclamation and theology rest on the 'religious *a priori*' of mankind. 'Christianity' has always been a form – perhaps the true form – of 'religion'. But if one day it becomes clear that this *a priori* does not exist at all, but was a historically conditioned and transient form of human self-expression, and if therefore man becomes radically religionless – and I think that that is already more or less the case (else how is it, for example, that this war, in contrast to all previous ones, is not calling forth any 'religious' reaction?) – what does that mean for 'Christianity'? It means that the foundation is taken away from the whole of what has up to now been our 'Christianity', and that there remain only a few 'last survivors of the age of chivalry', or a few intellectually dishonest people, on whom we can descend as 'religious'. Are they to be the chosen few? Is it on this dubious group of people that we are to pounce in fervour, pique, or indignation, in order to sell them our goods? Are we to fall upon a few unfortunate people in their hour of weakness and exercise a sort of religious compulsion on them? If we don't want to do all that, if our final judgment must be that the western form of Christianity, too, was only a preliminary stage to a complete absence of religion, what kind of situation emerges for us, for the church? How can Christ become the Lord of the religionless as well? Are there religionless Christians? If religion is only a garb of Christianity – and even this garb has looked very different at different times – then what is a religionless Christianity?

Barth, who is the only one to have started along this line of thought, did not carry it to completion, but arrived at a positivism of revelation, which in the last analysis is essentially conservatism For the religionless working man (or any other man) nothing decisive is gained here. The questions to be answered would surely be: What do a church, a community, a sermon, a liturgy, a Christian life mean in a religionless world? How do we speak of God – without religion, i.e. without the temporally conditioned presuppositions of metaphysics, inwardness, and so on? How do we speak (or perhaps we cannot now even 'speak' as we used to) in a 'worldly' way about 'God'? In what way are we 'religionless-worldly' Christians, in what way are we the *ek-klesia*, those who are called forth, not regarding ourselves from a religious point of view as specially favoured, but rather as belonging wholly to the world? In that case Christ is no longer an object of religion, but something quite different, really the Lord of the world. But what does that mean? What is the place of worship and prayer in a religionless situation? Does the secret discipline, or alternatively the difference (which I have suggested to you before) between penultimate and ultimate, take on a new importance here?

I must break off for today, so that the letter can go straight away. I'll write to you again about it in two days' time. I hope you see more or less what I mean, and that it doesn't bore you. Goodbye for the present. It's not easy always to write without an echo, and you must excuse me if that makes it something of a monologue...

I find, after all, that I can write a little more. – The Pauline question whether *peritome* [circumcision] is a condition of justification seems to me in present-day terms to be whether religion is a condition of salvation. Freedom from *peritome* is also freedom from religion. I often ask myself why a 'Christian instinct' often draws me more to the religionless people than to the religious, by which I don't in the least mean with any evangelizing intention, but, I might almost say, 'in brotherhood'. While I'm often reluctant to mention God by name to religious people – because that name somehow seems to me here not to ring true, and I feel myself to be slightly dishonest (it's particularly bad when others start to talk in religious jargon; I then dry up almost completely and feel awkward and uncomfortable) – to people with no religion I can on occasion mention him by name quite calmly and as a matter of course. Religious people speak of God when human knowledge (perhaps simply because they are too lazy to think) has come to an end, or when human resources fail – in fact it is always the *deus ex machina* that they bring on to the scene, either for the apparent solution of insoluble problems, or as strength in human failure – always, that is to say, exploiting human weakness or on human boundaries. Of necessity, that can go on only till people can by their own strength push these boundaries somewhat further out, so that God becomes superfluous as a *deus ex machina*. I've come to be doubtful of talking about any human boundaries (is even death, which people now hardly fear, and is sin, which they now hardly understand, still a genuine boundary today?). It always seems to me that we are trying anxiously in this way to reserve some space for God; I should like to speak of God not on the boundaries but at the centre, not in weaknesses but in strength; and therefore not in death and guilt but in man's life and goodness. On the boundaries, it seems to me better to be silent and leave the insoluble unsolved. Belief in the resurrection is *not* the 'solution' of the problem of death. God's 'beyond' is not the beyond of our cognitive faculties. The transcendence of epistemological theory has nothing to do with the transcendence of God. God is beyond in the midst of our life. The church stands, not on the boundaries where human powers give out, but in the middle of the village. That is how it is in the Old Testament, and in this sense we still read the New Testament far too little in the light of the Old. How this religionless Christianity looks, what form it takes, is something that I'm thinking about a great deal, and I shall be writing to you again about it soon. It may be that on us in particular, midway between East and West, there will fall a heavy responsibility.

Now I really must stop. It would be fine to have a word from you about all this; it would mean a great deal to me – probably more than you can imagine. Sometime, just read Prov. 22.11, 12; there is something that will bar the way to any escapism disguised as piety.

To Eberhard Bethge   5 May 1944

... A few more words about 'religionlessness'. I expect you remember Bultmann's essay on the 'demythologizing' of the New Testament? My view of it today would be, not that he went 'too far', as most people thought, but that he didn't go far enough. It's not only the 'mythological' concepts, such as miracle, ascension, and so on (which are not in principle separable from the concepts of God, faith, etc.), but 'religious' concepts generally, which are problematic. You can't, as Bultmann supposes, separate God and miracle, but you must be able to interpret and proclaim *both* in a 'non-religious' sense. Bultmann's approach is fundamentally still a liberal one (i.e. abridging the gospel), whereas I'm trying to think theologically.

What does it mean to 'interpret in a religious sense'? I think it means to speak on the one hand metaphysically, and on the other hand individualistically. Neither of these is relevant to the biblical message or to the man of today. Hasn't the individualistic question about personal salvation almost completely left us all? Aren't we really under the impression that there are more important things than that question (perhaps not more important than the *matter* itself, but more important than the *question*?)? I know it sounds pretty monstrous to say that. But, fundamentally, isn't this in fact biblical? Does the question about saving one's soul appear in the Old Testament at all? Aren't righteousness and the Kingdom of God on earth the focus of everything, and isn't it true that Rom. 3.24ff. is not an individualistic doctrine of salvation, but the culmination of the view that God alone is righteous? It is not with the beyond that we are concerned, but with this world as created and preserved, subjected to laws, reconciled, and restored. What is above this world is, in the gospel, intended to exist *for* this world; I mean that, not in the anthropocentric sense of liberal, mystic pietistic, ethical theology, but in the biblical sense of the creation and of the incarnation, crucifixion, and resurrection of Jesus Christ.

Barth was the first theologian to begin the criticism of religion, and that remains his really great merit; but he put in its place a positivist doctrine of revelation which says, in effect, 'Like it or lump it': virgin birth, Trinity, or anything else; each is an equally significant and necessary part of the whole, which must simply be swallowed as a whole or not at all. That isn't biblical. There are degrees of knowledge and degrees of significance; that means that a secret discipline must be restored whereby the *mysteries* of the Christian faith are protected against profanation. The positivism of revelation makes it too easy for itself, by setting up, as it does in the last analysis, a law of faith, and so mutilates what is – by Christ's incarnation! – a gift for us. In the place of religion there now stands the church – that is in itself biblical – but the world is in some degree made to depend on itself and left to its own devices, and that's the mistake.

I'm thinking about how we can reinterpret in a 'worldly' sense – in the sense of the Old Testament and of John 1.14 – the concepts of repentance, faith, justification, rebirth, and sanctification. I shall be writing to you about it again.

Forgive me for writing all this in German script; normally I do this only when my writing is for my own use – and perhaps what I've written was more to clear my own mind than to edify you. I really don't want to trouble you with problems, for you may well have no time to come to grips with them, and they may only bother you; but I can't help sharing my thoughts with you, simply because that is the best way to make them clear to myself. If that doesn't suit you at present, please say so.

[7 May 1944] Cantate

I've just heard some good morning-music by Reger and Hugo Distler; it was a good beginning for Sunday. The only jarring note was an interruption announcing that 'enemy air squadrons are moving towards ...' The connection between the two is not immediately obvious.

I thought last night about what mothers-in-law should do... I'm sure that they should not give advice; what right have they to undertake anything of the kind? It is their privilege to have a *grown-up* daughter or son, and they ought to regard that as an enrichment of their family, not as an occasion for criticism. They may find joy in their children, and give them help and advice if they're asked to, but the marriage completely relieves them of any responsibility for upbringing; that is really a privilege. I believe that when a mother-in-law sees that her child is really loved ... she should just be glad of it and let everything else take a back seat, especially any attempts to alter character! There are few people who know how to value reticence. I think mother and father can. The siren is just going; more later.

Well, it was pretty heavy again, and I'm always glad to know that Renate is out of Berlin. With regard to reticence, it all depends on *what* we are keeping to ourselves, and on whether there is one person with whom we can share everything ... I think it would be going too far to speak of the jealousy of mothers-in-law; it would be truer to say that there are two kinds of love, a mother's and a wife's; and that gives rise to a great deal of misunderstanding. Incidentally, it's much easier for sons-in-law than for daughters-in-law to get on peacefully with a mother-in-law – although the Bible gives a unique example to the contrary in Naomi and Ruth...

Your hope that leave may be near is also a great piece of good news for me. If you really manage to be together again in a few days – though in all these hopes one must always keep the joyful anticipation damped down a bit until the last minute – and if you can also have your child baptized then, I shouldn't like the thought of my absence to cast the least shadow on your happiness and particularly on you personally, Eberhard. I shall try to write you something for the occasion, and you know that all my thoughts will be with you. It's painful for me, to be sure, that the improbable has happened, and that I shall not be able to celebrate the day with you; but I've quite reconciled myself to it. I believe that nothing that happens to me is meaningless, and that it is good for us all that it should be so, even if it runs counter to our own wishes. As I see it, I'm here for some purpose, and I only hope I may fulfil it. In the light of the great purpose all our privations and disappointments are trivial. Nothing would be more unworthy and wrong-headed than to turn one of those rare occasions of joy, such as you're now experiencing, into a calamity because of my present situation. That would go entirely against the grain, and would undermine my optimism with regard to my case. However thankful we may be for all our personal pleasures, we mustn't for a moment lose sight of the great things that we're living for, and they must shed light rather than gloom on your joy. I couldn't bear to think that your few weeks of happiness, which you've had difficulty enough in getting, should be in the very least clouded by my present circumstances. That would be a real calamity, and the other is not. My only concern is to help you, as far as I can, to keep the lustre of these spring days – I expect you're celebrating your first wedding anniversary together – as radiant as may be. Please don't think for a moment that you're missing something through my not being with you – far from it! And above all, please don't think I'm finding it difficult to get these words out for your sake; on the contrary, they are my most earnest request for you, and its fulfilment would simply make me pleased and happy. If we did manage to meet while you're on leave, I should be only too delighted; but please don't put yourself out over it – I still have vivid memories of 23 December! And please don't lose a single day for the sake of spending a little time with me here. I know you would willingly do

94

so, but it would only distress me. Of course, if your father could arrange for you to visit me, as he did in December, I should be extremely grateful. Anyway, I know we shall be thinking of each other every morning as we read the daily texts, and I'm very glad you'll be able to read the Bible together again morning and evening; it will be a great help to you, not only for these present days, but for the future. Don't let the shortness of your time together and the thought that you must soon part overshadow the happiness of your leave. Don't try to do too much; let other people come and see you, instead of your going round everywhere to them, and enjoy every hour of the day peacefully as a great gift. My own opinion is that the next few weeks will bring such great and surprising events that when you start your leave you won't really know how it's all going to turn out. However much these events may affect our own personal destinies, I do hope they won't rob either of you of the peace and quietness that you need during your time together...

How I should have loved to baptize your little boy; but that's of no great consequence. Above all, I hope the baptism will help to assure you that your own lives, as well as the child's, are in safe keeping, and that you can face the future with confidence. Are you going to choose the text for the baptism yourself? If you're still looking for one, what about II Tim. 2.1, or Prov. 23.26 or 4.18? (I only came across the last of these recently; I think it's beautiful.)...

To Renate and Eberhard Bethge   18 May 1944

I very much wanted to write you something for the day of the baptism. It's not come out right. I'm sending it just to show you that I'm thinking very much about you. Thank you once again for choosing me as godfather for your child and for calling him after me. I hope you will always have specially happy memories of this day, and that it will give your short time together that essential quality that will endure across the time of your separation (which I trust will be brief). Some memories are painful, and others strengthen one; this day will strengthen you.

Who is baptizing him? Who will be sponsor? How will you celebrate it? I hope to hear everything soon, preferably from you yourselves. Please don't grieve over me. Martin [Niemöller] has had nearly seven years of it, and that is a very different matter...

Thoughts on the Day of the Baptism of
Dietrich Wilhelm Rüdiger Bethge
May 1944

You are the first of a new generation in our family, and therefore the oldest representative of your generation. You will have the priceless advantage of spending a good part of your life with the third and fourth generation that went before you. Your great-grandfather will be able to tell you, from his own personal memories, of people who were born in the eighteenth century; and one day, long after the year 2000, you will be the living bridge over which your descendants will get an oral tradition of more than 250 years – all this *sub conditione Jacobea*, 'if the Lord wills'. So your birth provides us with a suitable occasion to reflect on the changes that time brings, and to try to scan the outlines of the future.

The three names that you bear refer to three houses with which your life is, and always should be, inseparably connected. Your grandfather on your father's side lived in a country parsonage. A simple, healthy life, with wide intellectual interests, joy in the most homely things, a natural and unaffected interest in ordinary people and their work, a capacity for self-help in practical things, and a modesty grounded in spiritual contentment – those are the earthly values which were at home in the country parsonage, and which you will meet in your father. In all the circumstances of life you will find them a firm basis for living together with other people, and for achieving real success and inward happiness.

The urban middle-class culture embodied in the home of your mother's parents has led to pride in public service, intellectual achievement and leadership, and a deep-rooted sense of duty towards a great heritage and cultural tradition. This will give you, even before you are aware of it, a way of thinking and acting which you can never lose without being untrue to yourself.

It was a kindly thought of your parents that you should be known by the name of your great-uncle, who is a pastor and a great friend of your father's; he is at present sharing the fate of many other good Germans and Protestant Christians, and so he has only been able to participate at a distance in your parents' wedding and in your own birth and baptism, but he looks forward to your future with great confidence and cheerful hope. He is striving to keep up the spirit – as far as he understands it – that is embodied in his parents' (your great-grandparents') home. He takes it as a good omen for your future that it was in that home that your parents got to know each other, and he hopes that one day you will be thankful for its spirit and draw in the strength that it gives.

By the time you have grown up, the old country parsonage and the old town villa will belong to a vanished world. But the old spirit, after a time of misunderstanding and weakness, withdrawal and recovery, preservation and rehabilitation, will produce new forms. To be deeply rooted in the soil of the past makes life harder, but it also makes it richer and more vigorous. There are in human life certain fundamental truths to which men will always return sooner or later. So there is no need to hurry; we have to be able to wait. 'God seeks what has been driven away' (Eccles. 3.15).

In the revolutionary times ahead the greatest gift will be to know the security of a good home. It will be a bulwark against all dangers from within and without. The time when children broke away in arrogance from their parents will be past. Children will be drawn into their parents' protection, and they will seek refuge, counsel, peace, and enlightenment. You are lucky to have parents who know at first hand what it means to have a parental home in stormy times. In the general impoverishment of intellectual life you will find your parents' home a storehouse of spiritual values and a source of intellectual stimulation. Music, as your parents understand and practise it, will help to dissolve your perplexities and purify your character and sensibility, and in times of care and sorrow will keep a ground-bass of joy alive in you. Your parents will soon be teaching you to help yourself and never to be afraid of soiling your hands. The piety of your home will not be noisy or loquacious, but it will teach you to pray, to fear and love God above everything, and to do the will of Jesus Christ. 'My son, keep your father's commandment, and forsake not your mother's teaching. Bind them upon your heart always; tie them about your neck.

When you walk, they will lead you; when you lie down, they will watch over you; and when you awake, they will talk with you' (Prov. 6.20-22). 'Today salvation has come to this house' (Luke 19.9).

I wish you could grow up in the country; but it will not be the countryside in which your father grew up. People used to think that the big cities offered the fullest kind of life and lots of pleasure, and they used to flock to them as though to a festival; but those cities have now brought on themselves death and dying, with all imaginable horrors, and have become fearsome places from which women and children have fled. The age of big cities on our continent seems to have come to an end. According to the Bible, Cain founded the first city. It may be that a few world metropolises will survive, but their brilliance, however alluring it may be, will in any case have something uncanny about it for a European. On the other hand, the flight from the cities will mean that the countryside is completely changed. The peace and seclusion of country life have already been largely undermined by the radio, the car, and the telephone, and by the spread of bureaucracy into almost every department of life; and now if millions of people who can no longer endure the pace and the demands of city life are moving into the country, and if entire industries are dispersed into rural areas, then the urbanization of the country will go ahead fast, and the whole basic structure of life there will be changed. The village of thirty years ago no more exists today than the idyllic South Sea island. In spite of man's longing for peace and solitude, these will be difficult to find. But with all these changes, it will be an advantage to have under one's feet a plot of land from which to draw the resources of a new, natural, unpretentious, and contented day's work and evening's leisure. 'There is great gain in godliness and contentment;... if we have food and clothing, with these we shall be content' (I Tim. 6.6f.). 'Give me neither poverty nor riches; feed me with the food that is needful for me, lest I be full, and deny thee, and say, "Who is the Lord?", or lest I be poor, and steal, and profane the name of my God' (Prov. 30.8f.). 'Flee from the midst of Babylon... She was not healed... Forsake her, and let us go each to his own country' (Jer. 51.6, 9).

We have grown up with the experience of our parents and grand-parents that a man can and must plan, develop, and shape his own life, and that life has a purpose, about which a man must make up his mind, and which he must then pursue with all his strength. But we have learnt by experience that we cannot plan even for the coming day, that what we have built up is being destroyed over-night, and that our life, in contrast to that of our parents, has become formless or even fragmentary. In spite of that, I can only say that I have no wish to live in any other time than our own, even though it is so inconsiderate of our outward well-being. We realize more clearly than formerly that the world lies under the wrath and grace of God. We read in Jer. 45: 'Thus says the Lord: Behold, what I have built I am breaking down, and what I have planted I am plucking up... And do you seek great things for yourself? Seek them not; for, behold, I am bringing evil upon all flesh; ... but I will give your life as a prize of war in all places to which you may go.' If we can save our souls unscathed out of the wreckage of our material possessions, let us be satisfied with that. If the Creator destroys his own handiwork, what right have we to lament the destruction of ours? It will be the task of our generation, not to 'seek great things', but to save and preserve our souls out of the chaos, and to realize that it is the only thing we can carry as a 'prize' from the burning building. 'Keep your heart with all vigilance; for from it flows the spring of life' (Prov. 4.23). We shall have to keep our lives rather than shape them, to hope rather than plan, to hold out rather than march forward. But we do want to preserve for you, the rising generation, what will make it possible for you to plan, build up, and shape a new and better life.

We have spent too much time in thinking, supposing that if we weigh in advance the possibilities of any action it will happen automatically. We have learnt, rather too late, that action comes, not from thought, but from a readiness for responsibility. For you thought and action will enter on a new relationship; your thinking will be confined to your responsibilities in action. With us thought was often the luxury of the onlooker; with you it will be entirely subordinated to action. 'Not every one who *says* to me, "Lord, Lord", shall enter the kingdom of heaven, but he who *does* the will of my Father who is in heaven', said Jesus (Matt. 7.21).

For the greater part of our lives pain was a stranger to us. To be as free as possible from pain was unconsciously one of our guiding principles. Niceties of feeling, sensitivity to our own and other people's pain are at once the strength and the weakness of our way of life. From its early days your generation will be tougher and closer to real life, for you will have had to endure privation and pain, and your patience will have been greatly tried. 'It is good for a man that he bear the yoke in his youth' (Lam. 3.27).

We thought we could make our way in life with reason and justice, and when both failed, we felt that we were at the end of our tether. We have constantly exaggerated the importance of reason and justice in the course of history. You, who are growing up in a world war which ninety per cent of mankind did not want, but for which they have to risk losing their goods and their lives, are learning from childhood that the world is controlled by forces against which reason can do nothing; and so you will be able to cope with those forces more successfully. In our lives the 'enemy' did not really exist. You know that you have enemies and friends, and you know what they can mean in your life. You are learning very early in life ways (which we did not know) of fighting an enemy, and also the value of unreserved trust in a friend. 'Has not man a hard service upon earth?' (Job 7.1). 'Blessed be the Lord, my rock, who trains my hands for war, and my fingers for battle; my rock and my fortress, my stronghold and my deliverer, my shield and he in whom I take refuge' (Ps. 144.1f.). 'There is a friend who sticks closer than a brother' (Prov. 18.24).

Are we moving towards an age of colossal organizations and collective institutions, or will the desire of innumerable people for small, manageable, personal relationships be satisfied? Must they be mutually exclusive? Might it not be that world organizations themselves, with their wide meshes, will allow more scope for personal interests? Similarly with the question whether we are moving towards an age of the selection of the fittest, i.e. an aristo-cratic society, or to uniformity in all material and spiritual aspects of human life. Although there has been a very far-reaching equal-ization here, the sensitiveness in all ranks of society for the human values of justice, achievement, and courage could create a new selection of people who will be allowed the right to provide strong leadership. It will not be difficult for us to renounce our privileges, recognizing the justice of history. We may have to face events and changes that take no account of our wishes and our rights. But if so, we shall not give way to embittered and barren pride, but consciously submit to divine judgment, and so prove ourselves worthy to survive by identifying ourselves generously and unselfishly with the life of the community and the sufferings of our fellow-men. 'But any nation which will bring its neck under the yoke of the king of Babylon and serve him, I will leave on its own land, to till it and dwell there, says the Lord' (Jer. 27,11). 'Seek the welfare of the city . . . and pray to the Lord on its behalf' (Jer. 29.7). 'Come, my people, enter your chambers, and shut your doors behind you; hide yourselves for a little while until the wrath is past' (Isa. 26.20). 'For his anger is but for a moment, and his favour is for a lifetime. Weeping may tarry for the night, but joy comes with the morning' (Ps. 30.5).

Today you will be baptized a Christian. All those great ancient words of the Christian proclamation will be spoken over you, and the command of Jesus Christ to baptize will be carried out on you, without your knowing anything about it. But we are once again being driven right back to the beginnings of our understanding. Reconciliation and redemption, regeneration and the Holy Spirit, love of our enemies, cross and resurrection, life in Christ and Christian discipleship – all these things are so difficult and so remote that we hardly venture any more to speak of them. In the traditional words and acts we suspect that there may be something quite new and revolutionary, though we cannot as yet grasp or express it. That is our own fault. Our church, which has been fighting in these years only for its self-preservation, as though that were an end in itself, is incapable of taking the word of reconciliation and redemption to mankind and the world. Our earlier words are therefore bound to lose their force and cease, and our being Christians today will be limited to two things: prayer and righteous action among men. All Christian thinking, speaking, and organizing must be born anew out of this prayer and action. By the time you have grown up, the church's form will have changed greatly. We are not yet out of the melting-pot, and any attempt to help the church prematurely to a new expansion of its organization

101

will merely delay its conversion and purification. It is not for us to prophesy the day (though the day will come) when men will once more be called so to utter the word of God that the world will be changed and renewed by it. It will be a new language, perhaps quite non-religious, but liberating and redeeming – as was Jesus' language; it will shock people and yet overcome them by its power; it will be the language of a new righteousness and truth, proclaiming God's peace with men and the coming of his kingdom. 'They shall fear and tremble because of all the good and all the prosperity I provide for it' (Jer. 33.9). Till then the Christian cause will be a silent and hidden affair, but there will be those who pray and do right and wait for God's own time. May you be one of them, and may it be said of you one day, 'The path of the righteous is like the light of dawn, which shines brighter and brighter till full day' (Prov. 4.18).

To Eberhard Bethge   20 May [1944]

Once again this letter is intended only for you … I must say to begin with that everything that you told me has moved me so much that I couldn't stop thinking of it all day yesterday and had a restless night; I'm infinitely grateful to you for it; for it was a confirmation of our friendship, and moreover reawakens the spirit for life and for battle, and makes it stubborn, clear and hard. But I can't completely escape the feeling that there is a tension in you which you can't get rid of completely, and so I would like to help you as a brother. Accept it as it is intended. If a man loves, he wants to live, to live above all, and hates everything that represents a threat to his life. You hate the recollection of the last weeks, you hate the blue sky, because it reminds you of them, you hate the planes, etc. You want to live with Renate and be happy, and you have a good right to that. And indeed you must live, for the sake of Renate and the little – and also the big – Dietrich. You haven't the right to speak as your chief did recently. On the contrary, you couldn't be responsible for that at all. Sometime you must argue it out with him quite quietly; it is obvious what is necessary, but you mustn't act as a result of any personal emotion. There's always a danger in all strong, erotic love that one may lose what I might call

102

the polyphony of life. What I mean is that God wants us to love him eternally with our whole hearts – not in such a way as to injure or weaken our earthly love, but to provide a kind of *cantus firmus* to which the other melodies of life provide the counterpoint. One of these contrapuntal themes (which have their own complete independence but are yet related to the *cantus firmus*) is earthly affection. Even in the Bible we have the Song of Songs; and really one can imagine no more ardent, passionate, sensual love than is portrayed there (see 7.6). It's a good thing that the book is in the Bible, in face of all those who believe that the restraint of passion is Christian (where is there such restraint in the Old Testament?). Where the *cantus firmus* is clear and plain, the counterpoint can be developed to its limits. The two are 'undivided and yet distinct', in the words of the Chalcedonian Definition, like Christ in his divine and human natures. May not the attraction and importance of polyphony in music consist in its being a musical reflection of this christological fact and therefore of our *vita christiana*? This thought didn't occur to me till after your visit yesterday. Do you see what I'm driving at? I wanted to tell you to have a good clear *cantus firmus*; that is the only way to a full and perfect sound, when the counterpoint has a firm support and can't come adrift or get out of tune, while remaining a distinct whole in its own right. Only a polyphony of this kind can give life a wholeness and at the same time assure us that nothing calamitous can happen as long as the *cantus firmus* is kept going. Perhaps a good deal will be easier to bear in these days together, and possibly also in the days ahead when you're separated. Please, Eberhard, do not fear and hate the separation, if it should come again with all its dangers, but rely on the *cantus firmus*. – I don't know whether I've made myself clear now, but one so seldom speaks of such things...

To Eberhard Bethge   21 May 1944

I've just written the date of this letter as my share in the baptism and the preparations for it. At the same moment the siren went, and now I'm sitting in the sick-bay and hoping that today at any rate you will have no air raid. What times these are! What a baptism! And what memories for the years to come! What matters is that we should direct these memories, as it were, into the right spiritual channels, and so make them harder, clearer, and more defiant, which is a good thing. There is no place for sentimentality on a day like this. If in the middle of an air raid God sends out the gospel call to his kingdom in baptism, it will be quite clear what that kingdom is and what it means. It is a kingdom stronger than war and danger, a kingdom of power and authority, signifying eternal terror and judgment to some, and eternal joy and righteousness to others, not a kingdom of the heart, but one as wide as the earth, not transitory but eternal, a kingdom that makes a way for itself and summons men to itself to prepare its way, a kingdom for which it is worth while risking our lives.

The shooting is just beginning, but it doesn't seem likely to be very bad today. I should so like to hear you preaching in a few hours' time ... At eight this morning I heard a chorale prelude on 'What God does is well done' – a good beginning to the day; as I listened to it, I thought of you and my godson. I hadn't heard an organ for a long time, and the sound of it was like a refuge in time of trouble. I'm really very sad indeed that your letter to me as godfather has gone astray. I'm sure that you will have said a few very good and beneficial and encouraging words to me in it, and I would have been and am very grateful for them. Will it still be possible to find it? And will you write me a few words instead? I suppose you'll have to make an after-dinner speech today, and that you'll be thinking of me as you do so. I should very much like to hear what you said. The very fact that we so rarely say such words to one another makes one long for them from time to time. Do you understand that? Perhaps one feels it all the more strongly through being cut off from other people here. I used to take such things for granted, and in fact I still do, in spite of everything. Did you find here recently that it's now 'harder to speak' than before? I didn't. I only ask because you said this in a recent letter.

Perhaps you were surprised that yesterday's letter was on the one hand intended to say something to *you*, but on the other was itself so helpless. But isn't this what happens? One tries to help and is oneself the person most in need of help. What is said about the *cantus firmus* was written more for Renate's sake than for your own; i.e. for the sake of your shared life rather than because I felt that you didn't know it all well enough. The image of polyphony is still pursuing me. When I was rather distressed today at not being with you, I couldn't help thinking that pain and joy are also part of life's polyphony, and that they can exist independently side by side. The day before yesterday you said something to the effect that perhaps I had things better than I knew. Certainly, Eberhard, I'm in much less danger than you, and I would therefore give a great deal to be able to change places with you in this respect. That's not just empty speaking; it keeps entering into my prayers quite automatically; I've already seen more of life and experienced more than you ... but perhaps that is precisely why I'm more 'tired of life' than you may be. So the advantage that you see in my position is relatively small. Isn't it rather the case that you experience life in all its sides, in happiness and in danger, and that that is better than when one is to some degree cut off from the breath of life, as I am here? I certainly don't want to be pitied, and I don't want to grieve you in any way, but I do want you to be *glad* about what you have: it really *is* the polyphony of life (excuse this riding round on my little invention!). . . .

I'm still completely under the influence of your story. If only we could experience all this together! I would much prefer to be with you there than all alone here in 'security'! When I think how many dangers you've been through in your life ... and how until recently you've had tangible proofs of your preservation, and how good things have kept happening to you unexpectedly ... I'm quite at ease and believe that you are well taken care of in the plans of God. At times now you may only see death in your thoughts about the war, but if you do so, you underestimate the number of ways in which God operates. The hour of a man's death is determined, and it will find him no matter where he may turn. We must be ready for it. But

> He knows ten thousand ways
> To save us from death's power.
> He gives us food and meat,
> A boon in famine's hour.

That's something we mustn't forget. – Another alert.

To Eberhard Bethge   [26 May 1944]

... On the duties of godparents: in the old books the godparents often played a special part in a child's life. Growing children often want sympathy, kindness, and advice from grown-up people other than their parents; and the godparents are the people chosen by the parents to help in this way. The godparent has the right to give good advice, whereas the parents give orders. I didn't have any godparents of this kind ... but I can imagine that I would very much have liked to have had one and could have used one very well. Did you? But this is the direction in which I see one of my future duties as a godparent ... I would give boys chiefly male and girls chiefly female godparents...

To Eberhard Bethge   29 May 1944

I hope that, in spite of the alerts, you are enjoying to the full the peace and beauty of these warm, summer-like Whitsuntide days. One gradually learns to acquire an inner detachment from life's menaces – although 'acquire detachment' really sounds too negative, formal, artificial, and stoical; and it's perhaps more accurate to say that we assimilate these menaces into our life as a whole. I notice repeatedly here how few people there are who can harbour conflicting emotions at the same time. When bombers come, they are all fear; when there is something nice to eat, they are all greed; when they are disappointed, they are all despair; when they are successful, they can think of nothing else. They miss the fullness of life and the wholeness of an independent existence; everything objective and subjective is dissolved for them into fragments. By contrast, Christianity puts us into many different dimensions of life at the same time; we make room in ourselves, to some extent, for God and the whole world. We rejoice with those who rejoice, and weep with those who weep; we are anxious (– I was again interrupted just then by the alert, and am now sitting out of doors enjoying the sun–) about our life, but at the same time we must think about things much more important to us than life itself. When the alert goes, for instance; as soon as we turn our minds from worrying about our own safety to the task of helping other people to keep calm, the situation is completely changed; life isn't pushed back into a single dimension, but is kept multi-dimensional and polyphonous. What a deliverance it is to be able to *think*, and thereby remain multi-dimensional. I've almost made it a rule here, simply to tell people who are trembling under an air raid that it would be much worse for a small town. We have to get people out of their one-track minds; that is a kind of 'preparation' for faith, or something that makes faith possible, although really it's only faith itself that can make possible a multi-dimensional life, and so enable us to keep this Whitsuntide, too, in spite of the alarms.

At first I was a bit disconcerted, and perhaps even saddened, not to have a letter from anyone this Whitsuntide. Then I told myself that it was perhaps a good sign, as it meant that no one was worrying about me. It's a strange human characteristic that we like other people to be anxious about us – at least just a trifle anxious.

Weizsäcker's book *The World-View of Physics* is still keeping me very busy. It has again brought home to me quite clearly how wrong it is to use God as a stop-gap for the incompleteness of our knowledge. If in fact the frontiers of knowledge are being pushed further and further back (and that is bound to be the case), then God is being pushed back with them, and is therefore continually in retreat. We are to find God in what we know, not in what we don't know; God wants us to realize his presence, not in unsolved problems but in those that are solved. That is true of the relationship between God and scientific knowledge, but it is also true of the wider human problems of death, suffering, and guilt. It is now possible to find, even for these questions, human answers that take no account whatever of God. In point of fact, people deal with these questions without God (it has always been so), and it is simply not true to say that only Christianity has a solution for them. As to the idea of 'solving' problems, the Christian answers are in fact just as unconvincing – or convincing – as any others. Here again, God is no stop-gap; he must be recognized at the centre of life, not just when we are at the end of our resources; he wills to be recognized in life, and not just when death comes; in health and vigour, and not just in suffering; in our activities, and not just in sin. The ground for this lies in the revelation of God in Jesus Christ. He is the centre of life, and he certainly didn't 'come' to answer our unsolved problems. From the centre of life certain questions, and their answers, are seen to be wholly irrelevant (I'm thinking of the judgment pronounced on Job's friends). In Christ there are no 'Christian problems'. – Enough of this; I've just been disturbed again.

I'm sitting alone upstairs. Everything is quiet in the building; a few birds are still singing outside, and I can even hear the cuckoo in the distance. I find these long, warm evenings, which I'm now living through here for the second time, rather trying. I long to be outside, and if I were not so 'reasonable', I might do something foolish. I wonder whether we have become *too* reasonable. When you've deliberately suppressed every desire for so long, it may have one of two bad results: either it burns you up inside, or it all gets so bottled up that one day there is a terrific explosion. It is, of course, conceivable that one may become completely selfless, and I know better than anyone else that that hasn't happened to me. Perhaps you will say that one oughtn't to suppress one's desires, and I expect you would be right. But look, this evening for example I couldn't dare to give really full rein to my imagination and picture myself and Maria at your house, sitting in the garden by the water and talking together into the night, etc., etc. That is simply self-torture, and gives one physical pain. So I take refuge in thinking, in writing letters, in delighting in your good fortune, and curb my desires as a measure of self-protection. However paradoxical it may sound, it would be more selfless if I didn't need to be so afraid of my desires, and could give them free rein – but that is very difficult. – Just now I happened to hear Solveig's Song on the wireless in the sick-bay. It quite got hold of me. To wait loyally a whole lifetime – that is to triumph over the hostility of space, i.e. separation, and over time, i.e. the past. Don't you think that such loyalty is the only way to happiness, and that disloyalty leads to unhappiness? – Well, I shall go to bed now, in case we have another disturbed night.

To Eberhard Bethge   [presumably 2 June 1944]

... While you're in Italy I shall write to you about the Song of Songs. I must say I should prefer to read it as an ordinary love song, and that is probably the best 'christological' exposition. I must think again about Eph. 5. I hope that by now you have found something about Bultmann, if it has not been lost...

To Eberhard Bethge

I should be behaving like a shy boy if I concealed from you the fact that occasionally I feel led to try my hand at poetry. Up to now I've been keeping it dark from everyone, even Maria, who would be most concerned with it – simply because it was somehow painful to me and because I didn't know whether it wouldn't frighten her more than please her. You are the one . . . to whom I can talk with a certain matter-of-factness; I hope that if need be you will tick me off and tell me clearly not to meddle with it. So today I'm sending you a sample, first, because I think it would be silly to have any secrets from you, secondly, so that you can have something you didn't expect to read on your journey, and thirdly, because the subject of it is a good deal in your mind at the moment, and what I've written may be on the lines of what you're already thinking as you part from Renate. This dialogue with the past, the attempt to hold on to it and recover it, and above all, the fear of losing it, is the almost daily accompaniment of my life here; and sometimes, especially after brief visits, which are always followed by long partings, it becomes a theme with variations. To take leave of others, and to live on past memories, whether it was yesterday or last year (they soon melt into one), is my ever-recurring duty, and you yourself once wrote that saying good-bye goes very much against the grain. In this attempt of mine the crucial part is the last few lines. I'm inclined to think they are too brief – what do you think? Strangely enough, they came out in rhyme of their own accord. The whole thing was composed in a few hours, and I didn't try to polish it.

Now that I've talked about it to someone for the first time, I see that I can and must also send it to Maria. If some of the things in it frighten her, she must work out what is meant. I would be glad to hear a word from you about it. Perhaps I shall suppress these impulses in future, and use my time to better advantage; but that might well depend on your opinion. If you like, I'll send you some more to look at.

THE PAST

O happiness beloved, and pain beloved in heaviness,
you went from me.
What shall I call you? Anguish, life, blessedness,
part of myself, my heart – the past?
The door was slammed;
I hear your steps depart and slowly die away.
What now remains for me – torment, delight, desire?
This only do I know: that with you, all has gone.
But do you feel how I now grasp at you
and so clutch hold of you
that it must hurt you?
How I so rend you
that your blood gushes out,
simply to be sure that you are near me,
a life in earthly form, complete?
Do you divine my terrible desire
for my own suffering,
my eager wish to see my own blood flow,
only that all may not go under,
lost in the past?

Life, what have you done to me?
Why did you come? Why did you go?
Past, when you flee from me,
are you not still my past, my own?

As o'er the sea the sun sinks ever faster,
as if it moved towards the darkness,
so does your image sink and sink and sink
without a pause
into the ocean of the past,
and waves engulf it.
As the warm breath dissolves
in the cool morning air,
so does your image vanish from me,

and I no longer know
your face, your hands, your form.
There comes a smile, a glance, a greeting;
it fades, dissolves,
comfortless, distant,
is destroyed, is past.

I would inhale the fragrance of your being,
absorb it, stay with it,
as on hot summer days the heavy blossoms welcoming the bees
intoxicate them,
as privet makes the hawk-moths drunken –
but a harsh gust destroys both scent and blossoms,
and I stand like a fool
before the vanished past.

It is as if parts of my flesh were torn out with red-hot pincers,
when you, my past life, so quickly depart.
Raging defiance and anger beset me,
wild, useless questions I fling into the void.
'Why, why, why?' I keep on repeating –
why cannot my senses hold you,
life now passing, now past?
Thus I will think, and think anew,
until I find what I have lost.
But I feel
that everything around me, over, under me
is smiling at me, unmoved, enigmatic,
smiling at my quite hopeless efforts
to grasp the wind,
to capture what has gone.

Evil comes into my eye and soul;
what I see, I hate;
I hate what moves me;
all that lives I hate, all that is lovely,
all that would recompense me for my loss.
I want my life; I claim my own life back again,
my past, yourself.

Yourself. A tear wells up and fills my eye;
can I, in mists of tears,
regain your image,
yourself entire?
But I will not weep;
only the strong are helped by tears,
weaklings they make ill.

Wearily I come to the evening;
welcome are bed and oblivion
now that my own is denied me.
Night, blot out what separates, give me oblivion,
in charity perform your kindly office;
to you I trust myself.
But night is wise and mighty,
wiser than I, and mightier than day,
What no earthly power can do,
what is denied to thoughts and senses, to defiance, to tears,
night brings me, in its bounty overflowing.
Unharmed by hostile time,
pure, free, and whole,
you are brought to me by dream,
you, my past, my life,
you, the day and hour but lately gone.

Close to you I waken in the dead of night,
and start with fear –
are you lost to me once more? Is it always vainly that I seek you,
you, my past?
I stretch my hands out,
and I pray –
and a new thing now I hear:
'The past will come to you once more,
and be your life's most living part,
through thanks and repentance.
Feel in the past God's forgiveness and goodness,
pray him to keep you today and tomorrow.'

To Eberhard Bethge   6 June 1944

I'm sending you this hurried greeting, simply because I want in
some way to share the day with you yourself and with all of you.
The news didn't come as a surprise to me, and yet things turn out
differently from what we expect. Today's texts take us to the heart
of the gospel – 'redemption' is the key word to it all. Let us face the
coming weeks in faith and in great assurance about the general
future, and commit your way and all our ways to God. *Charis kai
eirene*! [Grace and peace!]

To Eberhard Bethge   8 June 1944

... You now ask so many important questions on the subjects that
have been occupying me lately, that I should be happy if I could
answer them myself. But it's all very much in the early stages
and, as usual, I'm being led on more by an instinctive feeling for
questions that will arise later than by any clarity that I've already
achieved about them. I'll try to define my position from the historical angle.

The movement that began about the thirteenth century (I'm not
going to get involved in any argument about the exact date)
towards the autonomy of man (which I should understand to
mean the discovery of the laws by which the world lives and
deals with itself in science, social and political life, art, ethics, and
religion) has in our time reached a degree of completion. Man has
learnt to deal with himself in all questions of importance without
recourse to the 'working hypothesis' called 'God'. In questions of
science, art, and ethics this has become an understood thing on
which one now hardly dares to touch. But for the last hundred
years or so it has also become increasingly true of religious questions; it is becoming evident that everything also gets along without 'God' – and, in fact, just as well as before. As in the scientific
field, so in human affairs generally, 'God' is being pushed more
and more out of life, losing more and more ground.

Roman Catholic and Protestant historians agree that it is in this
development that the great defection from God, from Christ, is to
be seen; and the more they claim and play off God and Christ
against it, the more the development considers itself to be anti-

113

Christian. The world that has become conscious of itself and the laws that govern its own existence has grown self-confident in what seems to us to be an uncanny way. False developments and failures do not make the world doubt the necessity of the course that it is taking, or of its development; they are accepted with fortitude and detachment as part of the bargain, and even an event like the present war is no exception. Christian apologetic has taken up varied forms of opposition to this self-assurance. Efforts are made to prove to the world come of age that it cannot live without the tutelage of 'God'. Even though there has been surrender on all worldly problems, there still remain the so-called 'ultimate questions' – death, guilt – to which only 'God' can give an answer, and because of which we need God and the church and the pastor. So we live, in some degree, on these so-called ultimate questions of humanity. But what if one day they no longer exist as such, if they too can be answered 'without God'? Of course, we now have the secularized offshoots of Christian theology, namely existentialist philosophy and the psychotherapists, who demonstrate to secure, contented, and happy mankind that it is really unhappy and desperate and simply unwilling to admit that it is in a predicament about which it knows nothing, and from which only they can rescue it. Wherever there is health, strength, security, simplicity, they scent luscious fruit to gnaw at or to lay their pernicious eggs in. They set themselves to drive people to inward despair, and then the game is in their hands. That is secularized methodism. And whom does it touch? A small number of intellectuals, of degenerates, of people who regard themselves as the most important thing in the world, and who therefore like to busy themselves with themselves. The ordinary man, who spends his everyday life at work and with his family, and of course with all kinds of diversions, is not affected. He has neither the time nor the inclination to concern himself with his existential despair, or to regard his perhaps modest share of happiness as a trial, a trouble, or a calamity.

The attack by Christian apologetic on the adulthood of the world I consider to be in the first place pointless, in the second place ignoble, and in the third place unchristian. Pointless, because it seems to me like an attempt to put a grown-up man back into adolescence, i.e. to make him dependent on things on which he is, in fact, no longer dependent, and thrusting him into problems that are, in fact, no longer problems to him. Ignoble, because it amounts to an attempt to exploit man's weakness for purposes that are alien to him and to which he has not freely assented. Unchristian, because it confuses Christ with one particular stage in man's religiousness, i.e. with a human law. More about this later.

But first, a little more about the historical position. The question is: Christ and the world that has come of age. The weakness of liberal theology was that it conceded to the world the right to determine Christ's place in the world; in the conflict between the church and the world it accepted the comparatively easy terms of peace that the world dictated. Its strength was that it did not try to put the clock back, and that it genuinely accepted the battle (Troeltsch), even though this ended with its defeat.

Defeat was followed by surrender, and by an attempt to make a completely fresh start based on the fundamentals of the Bible and the Reformation. Heim sought, along pietist and methodist lines, to convince the individual man that he was faced with the alternative 'despair or Jesus'. He gained 'hearts'. Althaus (carrying forward the modern and positive line with a strong confessional emphasis) tried to wring from the world a place for Lutheran teaching (ministry) and Lutheran worship, and otherwise left the world to its own devices. Tillich set out to interpret the evolution of the world (against its will) in a religious sense – to give it its shape through religion. That was very brave of him, but the world unseated him and went on by itself; he, too, sought to understand the world better than it understood itself; but it felt that it was completely misunderstood, and rejected the imputation. (Of course, the world *must* be understood better than it understands itself, but not 'religiously' as the religious socialists wanted.)

Barth was the first to realize the mistake that all these attempts (which were all, in fact, still sailing, though unintentionally, in the channel of liberal theology) were making in leaving clear a space for religion in the world or against the world. He brought in against religion the God of Jesus Christ, '*pneuma* against *sarx*'. That remains his greatest service (his *Epistle to the Romans*, second edition, in spite of all the neo-Kantian egg-shells). Through his later dogmatics, he enabled the church to effect this distinction, in principle, all along the line. It was not in ethics, as is often said, that

115

he subsequently failed – his ethical observations, as far as they exist, are just as important as his dogmatic ones –; it was that in the non-religious interpretation of theological concepts he gave no concrete guidance, either in dogmatics or in ethics. There lies his limitation, and because of it his theology of revelation has become positivist, a 'positivism of revelation'' as I put it.

The Confessing Church has now largely forgotten all about the Barthian approach, and has lapsed from positivism into conservative restoration. The important thing about that church is that it carries on the great concepts of Christian theology; but it seems as if doing this is gradually just about exhausting it. It is true that there are in those concepts the elements of genuine prophecy (among them two things that you mention: the claim to truth, and mercy) and of genuine worship; and to that extent the Confessing Church gets only attention, hearing, and rejection. But both of them remain undeveloped and remote, because there is no interpretation of them. Those who, like e.g. Schütz or the Oxford Group or the Berneucheners, miss the 'movement' and the 'life', are dangerous reactionaries; they are reactionary because they go right back behind the approach of the theology of revelation and seek for 'religious' renewal. They simply haven't understood the problem at all yet, and their talk is entirely beside the point. There is no future for them (though the Oxford Group would have the best chance if they were not so completely without biblical substance).

Bultmann seems to have somehow felt Barth's limitations, but he misconstrues them in the sense of liberal theology, and so goes off into the typical liberal process of reduction – the 'mythological' elements of Christianity are dropped, and Christianity is reduced to its 'essence'. My view is that the full content, including the 'mythological' concepts, must be kept – the New Testament is not a mythological clothing of a universal truth; this mythology (resurrection etc.) is the thing itself – but the concepts must be interpreted in such a way as not to make religion a precondition of faith (cf. Paul and circumcision). Only in that way, I think, will liberal theology be overcome (and even Barth is still influenced by it, though negatively) and at the same time its question be genuinely taken up and answered (as is *not* the case in the Confessing Church's positivism of revelation!). Thus the world's coming of

116

age is no longer an occasion for polemics and apologetics, but is now really better understood than it understands itself, namely on the basis of the gospel and in the light of Christ.

Now for your question whether there is any 'ground' left for the church, or whether that ground has gone for good; and the other question, whether Jesus didn't use men's 'distress' as a point of contact with them, and whether therefore the 'methodism' that I criticized earlier isn't right.

To Eberhard Bethge   21 June [1944]

... This morning we had the worst of all the air raids so far. For several hours my room was so dark with the cloud of smoke that hung over the city that I almost switched the light on. I've just heard that all is well at home...

It often seems hard to have to spend the beautiful long summer days here for the second time; but one just can't choose where one has to be. So we must keep on trying to find our way through the petty thoughts that irritate us, to the great thoughts that strengthen us. – I'm at present reading the quite outstanding book by W. F. Otto, the classics man at Königsberg, *The Gods of Greece*. To quote from his closing words, it's about 'this world of faith, which sprang from the wealth and depth of human existence, not from its cares and longings'. Can you understand my finding something very attractive in this theme and its treatment, and also – *horribile dictu* – my finding these gods, when they are so treated, less offensive than certain brands of Christianity? In fact, that I almost think I could claim these gods for Christ? The book is most helpful for my present theological reflections. By the way, there's a good deal about Cardano in Dilthey.

SORROW AND JOY

Sorrow and joy,
striking suddenly on our startled senses,
seem, at the first approach, all but impossible
of just distinction one from the other,
even as frost and heat at the first keen contact
burn us alike.

117

Joy and sorrow,
hurled from the height of heaven in meteor fashion,
flash in an arc of shining menace o'er us.
Those they touch are left
stricken amid the fragments
of their colourless, usual lives.

Imperturbable, mighty,
ruinous and compelling,
sorrow and joy
— summoned or all unsought for —
processionally enter.
Those they encounter
they transfigure, investing them
with strange gravity
and a spirit of worship.

Joy is rich in fears;
sorrow rich in sweetness.
Indistinguishable from each other
they approach us from eternity,
equally potent in their power and terror.

From every quarter
mortals come hurrying,
part envious, part awe-struck,
swarming, and peering
into the portent,
where the mystery sent from above us
is transmuting into the inevitable
order of earthly human drama.
What is joy? What is sorrow?

Time alone can decide between them,
when the immediate poignant happening
lengthens out to continuous wearisome suffering,
when the laboured creeping moments of daylight
slowly uncover the fullness of our disaster,
sorrow's unmistakable features.

Then do most of our kind,
sated, if only by the monotony
of unrelieved unhappiness,
turn away from the drama, disillusioned,
uncompassionate.

O you mothers and loved ones – then, ah, then
comes your hour, the hour for true devotion.
Then your hour comes, you friends and brothers!
Loyalty can change the face of sorrow,
softly encircle it with love's most gentle
unearthly radiance.

To Eberhard Bethge   27 June 1944

... I'm at present writing an exposition of the first three
commandments. I find No. 2 particularly difficult. The usual interpretation of idolatry as 'wealth, sensuality, and pride' seems to me
quite unbiblical. That is a piece of moralizing. Idols are *worshipped*,
and idolatry implies that people still worship something. But we
don't worship anything now, not even idols. In that respect we're
truly nihilists.

Now for some further thoughts about the Old Testament. Unlike
the other oriental religions, the faith of the Old Testament isn't a
religion of redemption. It's true that Christianity has always been
regarded as a religion of redemption. But isn't this a cardinal error,
which separates Christ from the Old Testament and interprets him
on the lines of the myths about redemption? To the objection that a
crucial importance is given in the Old Testament to redemption
(from Egypt, and later from Babylon – cf. Deutero-Isaiah) it may be
answered that the redemptions referred to here are *historical*, i.e.
on *this* side of death, whereas everywhere else the myths about
redemption are concerned to overcome the barrier of death. Israel
is delivered out of Egypt so that it may live before God as God's
people on earth. The redemption myths try unhistorically to find
an eternity after death. Sheol and Hades are no metaphysical

constructions, but images which imply that the 'past', while it still exists, has only a shadowy existence in the present.

The decisive factor is said to be that in Christianity the hope of resurrection is proclaimed, and that that means the emergence of a genuine religion of redemption, the main emphasis now being on the far side of the boundary drawn by death. But it seems to me that this is just where the mistake and the danger lie. Redemption now means redemption from cares, distress, fears, and longing, from sin and death, in a better world beyond the grave. But is this really the essential character of the proclamation of Christ in the gospels and by Paul? I should say it is not. The difference between the Christian hope of resurrection and the mythological hope is that the former sends a man back to his life on earth in a wholly new way which is even more sharply defined than it is in the Old Testament. The Christian, unlike the devotees of the redemption myths, has no last line of escape available from earthly tasks and difficulties into the eternal, but, like Christ himself ('My God, why hast thou forsaken me?'), he must drink the earthly cup to the dregs, and only in his doing so is the crucified and risen Lord with him, and he crucified and risen with Christ. This world must not be prematurely written off; in this the Old and New Testaments are at one. Redemption myths arise from human boundary-experiences, but Christ takes hold of a man at the centre of his life.

You see how my thoughts are constantly revolving round the same theme. Now I must substantiate them in detail from the New Testament; that will follow later.

To Eberhard Bethge   30 June 1944

Today was a hot summer's day here, and I could enjoy the sun only with mixed feelings, as I can imagine what ordeals you're having to go through. Probably you're stuck somewhere or other, tired and up to your eyes in dust and sweat, and perhaps with no chance of washing or cooling down. I suppose you sometimes almost loathe the sun. And yet, you know, I should like to feel the full force of it again, making the skin hot and the whole body glow, and reminding me that I'm a corporeal being. I should like to be tired by the sun, instead of by books and thoughts. I should like to have it awaken my animal existence – not the kind that degrades a man, but the kind that delivers him from the stuffiness and artificiality of a purely intellectual existence and makes him purer and happier. I should like, not just to see the sun and sip at it a little, but to experience it bodily. Romantic sun-worshipping that just gets intoxicated over sunrise and sunset, while it knows something of the power of the sun, does not know it as a reality, but only as a symbol. It can never understand why people worshipped the sun as a god; to do so one needs experience, not only of light and colours, but also of heat. The hot countries, from the Mediterranean to India and Central America, have been the really intellectually creative countries. The colder lands have lived on the intellectual creativeness of the others, and anything original that they have produced, namely technology, serves in the last resort the material needs of life rather than the mind. Isn't that what repeatedly draws us to the hot countries? And may not such thoughts do something to compensate for the discomforts of the heat? . . .

A few hours ago Uncle Paul called here to inquire personally about my welfare. It's most comical how everyone goes about flapping his wings and – with a few notable exceptions – tries to outdo everyone else in undignified ways. It's painful, but some of them are in such a state now that they can't help it.

Now I will try to go on with the theological reflections that I broke off not long since. My starting point was that God is being increasingly pushed out of a world that has come of age, out of the spheres of our knowledge and life, and that since Kant he has only retained a place beyond the world of experience. Theology has on the one hand resisted this development with apologetics, and has taken up arms – in vain – against Darwinism, etc. On the other hand, it has accommodated itself to the development by letting God function only in the so-called ultimate questions as a *deus ex machina*; that means that he becomes the answer to life's problems, and the solution of its needs and conflicts. So where anyone has no such difficulties, or refuses to go into these things, to allow others to sympathize with him, then really he cannot be open to God; or else he must be shown that he is, in fact, deeply involved in such problems, needs, and conflicts, without admitting or knowing it. If that can be done – and existentialist philosophy and psychotherapy have worked out some quite ingenious methods in that direction – then this man can now be claimed for God, and methodism can celebrate its triumph. But if he cannot be brought to see and admit that his happiness is really an evil, his health sickness, and his vigour despair, the theologian is at his wits' end. It's a case of having to do either with a hardened sinner of a particularly ugly type, or with a man of 'bourgeois complacency', and the one is as far from salvation as the other.

You see, that is the attitude that I am contending against. When Jesus blessed sinners, they were real sinners, but Jesus did not make everyone a sinner first. He called them away from their sin, not into their sin. It is true that encounter with Jesus meant the reversal of all human values. So it was in the conversion of Paul, though in his case the encounter with Jesus preceded the realization of sin. It is true that Jesus cared about people on the fringe of human society, such as harlots and tax-collectors, but never about them alone, for he sought to care about man as such. Never did he question a man's health, vigour, or happiness, regarded in themselves, or regard them as evil fruits; else why should he heal the sick and restore strength to the weak? Jesus claims for himself and the Kingdom of God the whole of human life in all its manifestations.

Of course I have to be interrupted just now! Let me just summarize briefly what I'm concerned about – the claim by Jesus Christ of a world that has come of age.

I can't write any more today, or else the letter will be kept here another week, and I don't want that to happen. So: To be continued!

Uncle Paul has been here. He had me brought downstairs at once, and stayed – Maetz and Maass were there – more than five hours! He had four bottles of *Sekt* brought – a unique event in the annals of this place – and was nicer and more generous than I should ever have expected. He probably wanted to make it ostentatiously clear what good terms he is on with me, and what he expects from the jittery and pedantic M. Such independence, which would be quite unthinkable in a civilian, impressed me greatly. By the way, he told me this story: At St Privat a wounded ensign shouted loudly, 'I am wounded; long live the king.' Thereupon General von Löwenfeld, who was also wounded, said 'Be quiet, ensign; we die here in silence!' – I am curious to know what will be the effect of his visit here; I mean what people will think of it.

8 July 1944

A little while ago I wrote you a letter with some very theoretical philosophy about heat. In the last few days I've been experiencing it on my own body. I feel as if I were in an oven, and I'm wearing only a shirt that I once brought you from Sweden, and a pair of shorts (has someone really walked off somewhere with your shirts? I'm sure that you will get them back again later), and the only reason why I don't complain about it is that I can imagine how badly you must be suffering from the heat, and how frivolous my former letter must have seemed to you. So I will try to squeeze a few thoughts out of my sweating brain, and let you have them. Who knows – it may be that it won't have to be too often now, and that we shall see each other sooner than we expect. The other day I read a fine and striking remark in Euripides, in a scene of reunion after a long separation – 'So, then, to meet again is a god.'

Now for a few more thoughts on our theme. Marshalling the biblical evidence needs more lucidity and concentration than I can command today. Wait a few more days, till it gets cooler! I haven't forgotten, either, that I owe you something about the non-religious interpretation of biblical concepts. But for today, here are a few preliminary remarks:

The displacement of God from the world, and from the public part of human life, led to the attempt to keep his place secure at least in the sphere of the 'personal', the 'inner', and the 'private'. And as every man still has a private sphere somewhere, that is where he was thought to be the most vulnerable. The secrets known to a man's valet – that is, to put it crudely, the range of his intimate life, from prayer to his sexual life – have become the hunting-ground of modern pastoral workers. In that way they resemble (though with quite different intentions) the dirtiest gutter journalists – do you remember the *Wahrheit* and the *Glocke*, which made public the most intimate details about prominent people? In the one case it's social, financial, or political blackmail and in the other, religious blackmail. Forgive me, but I can't put it more mildly.

From the sociological point of view this is a revolution from

123

below, a revolt of inferiority. Just as the vulgar mind isn't satisfied till it has seen some highly placed personage 'in his bath', or in other embarrassing situations, so it is here. There is a kind of evil satisfaction in knowing that everyone has his failings and weak spots. In my contacts with the 'outcasts' of society, its 'pariahs', I've noticed repeatedly that mistrust is the dominant motive in their judgment of other people. Every action, even the most un-selfish, of a person of high repute is suspected from the outset. These 'outcasts' are to be found in all grades of society. In a flower-garden they grub around only for the dung on which the flowers grow. The more isolated a man's life, the more easily he falls a victim to this attitude.

There is also a parallel isolation among the clergy, in what one might call the 'clerical' sniffing-around-after-people's-sins in order to catch them out. It's as if you couldn't know a fine house till you had found a cobweb in the furthest cellar, or as if you couldn't adequately appreciate a good play till you had seen how the actors behave off-stage. It's the same kind of thing that you find in the novels of the last fifty years, which do not think they have depicted their characters properly till they have described them in their marriage-bed, or in films where undressing scenes are thought necessary. Anything clothed, veiled, pure, and chaste is presumed to be deceitful, disguised, and impure; people here simply show their own impurity. A basic anti-social attitude of mistrust and suspicion is the revolt of inferiority.

Regarded theologically, the error is twofold. First, it is thought that a man can be addressed as a sinner only after his weaknesses and meannesses have been spied out. Secondly, it is thought that a man's essential nature consists of his inmost and most intimate background; that is defined as his 'inner life', and it is precisely in those secret human places that God is now said to have his domain!

On the first point it is to be said that man is certainly a sinner, but is far from being mean or common on that account. To put it rather tritely, were Goethe and Napoleon sinners because they weren't always faithful husbands? It's not the sins of weakness, but the sins of strength, which matter here. It's not in the least necessary to spy out things; the Bible never does so. (Sins of strength: in the genius, *hybris*; in the peasant, the breaking of the order of life – is

124

the decalogue a peasant ethic? –; in the bourgeois, fear of free responsibility. Is this correct?)

On the second point: the Bible does not recognize our distinction between the outward and the inward. Why should it? It is always concerned with *anthropos teleios*, the *whole* man, even where, as in the Sermon on the Mount, the decalogue is pressed home to refer to 'inward disposition'. That a good 'disposition' can take the place of total goodness is quite unbiblical. The discovery of the so-called inner life dates only from the Renaissance, probably from Petrarch. The 'heart' in the biblical sense is not the inner life, but the whole man as he is before God. But as man lives just as much from 'outwards' to 'inwards' as from 'inwards' to 'outwards', the view that his nature can be understood only from his intimate spiritual background is wholly erroneous.

My concern, therefore, is that God shouldn't be smuggled into some last secret place, but that we should frankly recognize that the world, and people, have come of age, that we shouldn't run man down in his worldliness, but confront him with God at his strongest point, that we should give up all our clerical tricks, and not regard psychotherapy and existentialist philosophy as God's pioneers. The importunity of all these methods is far too unaristo-cratic for the Word of God to ally itself with them. The Word of God is not allied with this revolt of mistrust, this revolt from below. On the contrary it reigns.

Well, now would be the time to say something concrete about the worldly interpretation of biblical concepts; but it's *too* hot!...

By the way, it would be very nice if you didn't throw away my theological letters but sent them on to Renate from time to time, as I'm sure they're too much of a burden for you. Perhaps I might want to read them again later for my work. One writes some things more freely and more vividly in a letter than in a book, and often I have better thoughts in a conversation by correspondence than by myself.

WHO AM I?

Who am I? They often tell me
I would step from my cell's confinement
calmly, cheerfully, firmly,
like a squire from his country-house.

Who am I? They often tell me
I would talk to my warders
freely and friendly and clearly,
as though it were mine to command.

Who am I? They also tell me
I would bear the days of misfortune
equably, smilingly, proudly,
like one accustomed to win.

Am I then really all that which other men tell of?
Or am I only what I know of myself,
restless and longing and sick, like a bird in a cage,
struggling for breath, as though hands were compressing my
    throat,
hungry for colours, for flowers, for the voices of birds,
thirsty for words of kindness, for neighbourliness,
trembling with anger at despotisms and petty humiliation,
caught up in expectation of great events,
powerlessly grieving for friends at an infinite distance,
weary and empty at praying, at thinking, at making,
faint, and ready to say farewell to it all?

Who am I? This or the other?
Am I one person today, and tomorrow another?
Am I both at once? A hypocrite before others,
and before myself a contemptibly woebegone weakling?
Or is something within me still like a beaten army,
fleeing in disorder from victory already achieved?

Who am I? They mock me, these lonely questions of mine.
Whoever I am, thou knowest, O God, I am thine.

CHRISTIANS AND PAGANS

1 Men go to God when they are sore bestead,
  Pray to him for succour, for his peace, for bread,
  For mercy for them sick, sinning, or dead;
  All men do so, Christian and unbelieving.

2 Men go to God when he is sore bestead,
  Find him poor and scorned, without shelter or bread,
  Whelmed under weight of the wicked, the weak, the dead;
  Christians stand by God in his hour of grieving.

3 God goes to every man when sore bestead,
  Feeds body and spirit with his bread;
  For Christians, pagans alike he hangs dead,
  And both alike forgiving.

To Eberhard Bethge   16 July [1944]

I heard yesterday from my parents that you had been moved
again. I hope to hear soon how you're getting on. The historic
atmosphere sounds attractive, anyway. Only ten years ago we
should hardly have realized that the symbolic crozier and ring,
claimed by both emperor and pope, could lead to an international
political struggle. Weren't they really *adiaphora*? We have had to
learn again, through our own experience, that they were not.
Whether Henry IV's pilgrimage to Canossa was sincere or merely
diplomatic, the picture of Henry IV in January 1077 has left its mark
permanently on the thought of European peoples. It was more
effective than the Concordat of Worms of 1122, which formally
settled the matter on the same lines. We were taught at school that
all these great disputes were a misfortune to Europe, whereas in
point of fact they are the source of the intellectual freedom that has
made Europe great.

There's not much to report about myself. I heard lately on the
wireless (not for the first time) some scenes from Carl Orff's operas
(and also *Carmina Burana*). I liked them very much; they were so
fresh, clear and bright. He has produced an orchestral version of
Monteverdi. Did you know that? I also heard a *concerto grosso* by
Handel, and was again quite surprised by his ability to give such

wide and immediate consolation in the slow movement, as in the *Largo*, in a way in which we wouldn't dare to any more. Handel seems to be more concerned than Bach with the effect of his music on the audience; that may be why he sometimes has a façade-like effect. Handel, unlike Bach, has a deliberate purpose behind his music. Do you agree?

I am very interested to read *The House of the Dead*, and I'm impressed by the non-moral sympathy that those outside have for its inhabitants. May not this amorality, the product of religiosity, be an essential trait of these people, and also help us to understand more recent events? For the rest, I'm doing as much writing and composing as much poetry as my strength allows. I've probably told you before that I often get down to a bit of work [listening to foreign broadcasts] in the evening, as we used to. Of course, I find that pleasant and useful...

If you have to preach in the near future, I should suggest taking some such text as Ps. 62.1; 119.94a; 42.5; Jer. 31.3; Isa. 41.10; 43.1; Matt. 28.20b; I should confine myself to a few simple but vital thoughts. One has to live for some time in a community to understand how Christ is 'formed' in it (Gal. 4.19); and that is especially true of the kind of community that you would have. If I can help in any way, I should be glad to.

Now for a few more thoughts on our theme. I'm only gradually working my way to the non-religious interpretation of biblical concepts; I can see the problem, but solving it is a different matter. On the historical side: There is one great development that leads to the world's autonomy. In theology one sees it first in Lord Herbert of Cherbury, who maintains that reason is sufficient for religious knowledge. In ethics it appears in Montaigne and Bodin with their substitution of rules of life for the commandments. In politics Machiavelli detaches politics from morality in general and founds the doctrine of 'reasons of state'. Later, and very differently from Machiavelli, but tending like him towards the autonomy of human society, comes Grotius, setting up his natural law as international law, which is valid *etsi deus non daretur*, 'even if there were no God'. The philosophers provide the finishing touches: on the one hand we have the deism of Descartes, who holds that the world is a mechanism, running by itself with no interference from God; and on the other hand the pantheism of Spinoza, who says that God is nature. In the last resort, Kant is a deist, and Fichte and Hegel are pantheists. Everywhere the thinking is directed towards the autonomy of man and the world.

(It seems that in the natural sciences the process begins with Nicolas of Cusa and Giordano Bruno and the 'heretical' doctrine of the infinity of the universe. The classical *cosmos* was finite, like the created world of the Middle Ages. An infinite universe, however it may be conceived, is self-subsisting, *etsi deus non daretur*. It is true that modern physics is not as sure as it was about the infinity of the universe, but it has not gone back to the earlier conceptions of its finitude).

God as a working hypothesis in morals, politics, or science, has been surmounted and abolished; and the same thing has happened in philosophy and religion (Feuerbach!). For the sake of intellectual honesty, that working hypothesis should be dropped, or as far as possible eliminated. A scientist or physician who sets out to edify is a hybrid.

Anxious souls will ask what room there is left for God now; and as they know of no answer to the question, they condemn the whole development that has brought them to such straits. I wrote to you before about the various emergency exits that have been contrived; and we ought to add to them the *salto mortale* [death-leap] back into the Middle Ages. But the principle of the Middle Ages is heteronomy in the form of clericalism; a return to that can be a counsel of despair, and it would be at the cost of intellectual honesty. It's a dream that reminds one of the song *O wüsst' ich doch den Weg zurück, den weiten Weg ins Kinderland*. There is no such way – at any rate not if it means deliberately abandoning our mental integrity; the only way is that of Matt. 18.3, i.e. through repentance, through *ultimate* honesty.

And we cannot be honest unless we recogize that we have to live in the world *etsi deus non daretur*. And this is just what we do recognize – before God! God himself compels us to recognize it. So our coming of age leads us to a true recognition of our situation before God. God would have us know that we must live as men who manage our lives without him. The God who is with us is the God who forsakes us (Mark 15.34). The God who lets us live in the world without the working hypothesis of God is the God before whom we stand continually. Before God and with God we live

129

without God. God lets himself be pushed out of the world on to the cross. He is weak and powerless in the world, and that is precisely the way, the only way, in which he is with us and helps us. Matt. 8.17 makes it quite clear that Christ helps us, not by virtue of his omnipotence, but by virtue of his weakness and suffering.

Here is the decisive difference between Christianity and all religions. Man's religiosity makes him look in his distress to the power of God in the world: God is the *deus ex machina*. The Bible directs man to God's powerlessness and suffering; only the suffering God can help. To that extent we may say that the development towards the world's coming of age outlined above, which has done away with a false conception of God, opens up a way of seeing the God of the Bible, who wins power and space in the world by his weakness. This will probably be the starting-point for our 'worldly interpretation'.

18 July

I wonder whether any letters have been lost in the raids on Munich. Did you get the one with the two poems? It was just sent off that evening, and it also contained a few introductory remarks on our theological theme. The poem about Christians and pagans contains an idea that you will recognize: 'Christians stand by God in his hour of grieving'; that is what distinguishes Christians from pagans. Jesus asked in Gethsemane, 'Could you not watch with me one hour?' That is a reversal of what the religious man expects from God. Man is summoned to share in God's sufferings at the hands of a godless world.

He must therefore really live in the godless world, without attempting to gloss over or explain its ungodliness in some religious way or other. He must live a 'worldly' life, and thereby share in God's sufferings. He *may* live a 'worldly' life (as one who has been freed from false religious obligations and inhibitions). To be a Christian does not mean to be religious in a particular way, to make something of oneself (a sinner, a penitent, or a saint) on the basis of some method or other, but to be a man – not a type of man, but the man that Christ creates in us. It is not the religious act that makes the Christian, but participation in the sufferings of God in the secular life. That is *metanoia*: not in the first place thinking about one's own needs, problems, sins, and fears, but allowing oneself to be caught up into the way of Jesus Christ, into the messianic event, thus fulfilling Isa. 53 now. Therefore 'believe in the gospel', or, in the words of John the Baptist, 'Behold, the Lamb of God, who takes away the sin of the world' (John 1.29). (By the way, Jeremias has recently asserted that the Aramaic word for 'lamb' may also be translated 'servant'; very appropriate in view of Isa. 53!)

This being caught up into the messianic sufferings of God in Jesus Christ takes a variety of forms in the New Testament. It appears in the call to discipleship, in Jesus' table-fellowship with sinners, in 'conversions' in the narrower sense of the word (e.g. Zacchaeus), in the act of the woman who was a sinner (Luke 7) – an act that she performed without any confession of sin – in the healing of the sick (Matt. 8.17; see above), in Jesus' acceptance of children. The shepherds, like the wise men from the East, stand at the crib, not as 'converted sinners', but simply because they are drawn to the crib by the star just as they are. The centurion of Capernaum (who makes no confession of sin) is held up as a model of faith (cf. Jairus). Jesus 'loved' the rich young man. The eunuch (Acts 8) and Cornelius (Acts 10) are not standing at the edge of an abyss. Nathaniel is 'an Israelite indeed, in whom there is no guile' (John 1.47). Finally, Joseph of Arimathea and the women at the tomb. The only thing that is common to all these is their sharing in the suffering of God in Christ. That is their 'faith'. There is nothing of religious method here. The 'religious act' is always something partial; 'faith' is something whole, involving the whole of one's life. Jesus calls men, not to a new religion, but to life.

But what does this life look like, this participation in the power-lessness of God in the world? I will write about that next time, I hope. Just one more point for today. When we speak of God in a 'non-religious' way, we must speak of him in such a way that the godlessness of the world is not in some way concealed, but rather revealed, and thus exposed to an astonishing light. The world that has come of age is more godless, and perhaps for that very reason nearer to God, than the world before its coming of age. Forgive me for still putting it all so terribly clumsily and badly, as I really feel I am. But perhaps you will help me again to make things clearer and simpler, even if only by being able to talk about them with you and to hear you, so to speak, keep asking and answering...

All I want to do today is to send you a short greeting. I expect you are often with us here in your thoughts and are always glad of any sign of life, even if the theological discussion stops for a moment. These theological thoughts are, in fact, always occupying my mind; but there are times when I am just content to let life and faith carry me along without reflecting on them. At those times I simply take pleasure in the day's readings – in particular those of yesterday and today; and I'm always glad to go back to Paul Gerhardt's beautiful hymns.

During the last year or so I've come to know and understand more and more the profound this-worldliness of Christianity. The Christian is not a *homo religiosus*, but simply a man, as Jesus was a man – in contrast, shall we say, to John the Baptist. I don't mean the shallow and banal this-worldliness of the enlightened, the busy, the comfortable, or the lascivious, but the profound this-worldliness, characterized by discipline and the constant knowledge of death and resurrection. I think Luther lived a this-worldly life in this sense.

I remember a conversation that I had in America thirteen years ago with a young French pastor. We were asking ourselves quite simply what we wanted to do with our lives. He said he would like to become a saint (and I think it's quite likely that he has become one). At the time I was very impressed, but I disagreed with him, and said, in effect, that I should like to learn to have faith. For a long time I didn't realize the depth of the contrast. I thought I could acquire faith by trying to live a holy life, or something like it. I suppose I wrote *The Cost of Discipleship* as the end of that path. Today I can clearly see the dangers of that book, though I still stand by what I wrote.

I discovered later, and I'm still discovering right up to this moment, that it is only by living completely in this world that one learns to have faith. One must completely abandon any attempt to make something of oneself, whether it be a saint, or a converted sinner, or a churchman (a so-called priestly type!), a righteous man or an unrighteous one, a sick man or a healthy one. That is what I call this-worldliness: living unreservedly in life's duties, problems, successes and failures, experiences and perplexities. In so doing we throw ourselves completely into the arms of God, taking seriously, not our own sufferings, but those of God in the world – watching with Christ in Gethsemane. That, I think, is faith; that is *metanoia*; and that is how one becomes human and a Christian (cf. Jer. 45!). How can success make us arrogant, or failure lead us astray, when we share in God's sufferings through a life in this world?

You will see what I mean, even though I put it so briefly. I'm glad to have been able to learn this, and I know I've been able to do so only along the road that I've travelled. So I'm grateful for the past and present, and content with them.

You may be surprised at such a personal letter; but if for once I want to say this kind of thing, to whom should I say it? Perhaps the time will come one day when I can talk to Maria like this; I very much hope so. But I can't expect it of her yet.

May God in his mercy lead us through these times; but above all may he lead us to himself...

STATIONS ON THE ROAD TO FREEDOM

Discipline

If you set out to seek freedom, then learn above all things
discipline over your soul and your senses, lest passions and
   instincts
lead you now hither, now thither, in random directions.
Chaste be your mind and your body, completely subjected,
and in obedience seeking the aim set before them;
none learns the mystery of freedom with discipline lost.

Action

Daring to do what is right, not what fancy may tell you,
seizing reality boldly, not weighing up chances,
freedom's in action alone, not in wavering thought.
Leave aside anxious delay and go into the storm of our history,
borne along solely by faith and God's will and commandment;
freedom, exultant, will welcome your spirit with joy.

133

Suffering

Wonderful transformation. Your hands, so strong and active,
are bound; helpless and lonely you now see your action
ended; you sigh in relief, the right committing
calmly into a stronger hand; and rest content.
Just for a moment you blissfully touched upon freedom,
then, that it might be perfected in glory, you gave it to God.

Death

Come now, thou greatest of feasts on the journey to freedom
    eternal;
death, cast aside all the burdensome chains, and demolish
the walls of our temporal body, the walls of our soul which is
    blinded,
so that at last we may gaze upon that which here is begrudged us.
Freedom, how long we have sought thee in discipline, action and
    suffering;
dying, we know thee now in the visage of God.

To Eberhard Bethge   25 July 1944

... I've now finished *Memoirs from the House of the Dead*. It contains
a great deal that is wise and good. I'm still thinking about the
assertion, which in his case is certainly not a mere conventional
dictum, that man cannot live without hope, and that men who
have really lost all hope often become wild and wicked. It may
be an open question whether in this case hope = illusion. The
importance of illusion to one's life should certainly not be under-
estimated; but for a Christian there must be hope based on a firm
foundation. And if even illusion has so much power in people's
lives that it can keep life moving, how great a power there is in a
hope that is based on certainty, and how invincible a life with such
a hope is. 'Christ our hope' – this Pauline formula is the strength of
our lives...

To Eberhard Bethge [postmark 27 July 1944]

... Your summary of our theological theme is very clear and simple. The question how there can be a 'natural piety' is at the same time the question of 'unconscious Christianity', with which I'm more and more concerned. Lutheran dogmatists distinguished between a *fides directa* and a *fides reflexa*. They related this to the so-called children's faith, at baptism. I wonder whether this doesn't raise a far-reaching problem. I hope we shall soon come back to it.

To Eberhard Bethge 28 July [1944]

... You think the Bible hasn't much to say about health, fortune, vigour, etc. I've been thinking over that again. It's certainly not true of the Old Testament. The intermediate theological category between God and human fortune in the Old Testament is, as far as I can see, that of blessing. In the Old Testament – e.g. among the patriarchs – there's a concern not for fortune, but for God's blessing, which includes in itself all earthly good. In that blessing the whole of the earthly life is claimed for God, and it includes all his promises. Once again, it would be in accord with the usual spiritualized view of the New Testament to regard the Old Testament blessing as superseded in the New. But is it an accident that sickness and death are mentioned in connection with with misuse of the Lord's Supper ('The cup of *blessing*', I Cor. 10.16; 11.30), that Jesus restored people's health, and that while his disciples were with him they 'lacked nothing'? Now, is it right to set the Old Testament blessing against the cross? That is what Kierkegaard did. That makes the cross, or at least suffering, a principle; and that is just what gives rise to an unhealthy methodism, which deprives suffering of its character of contingency, of being sent by God. It's true that in the Old Testament the person who receives the blessing has to endure a great deal of suffering (e.g. Abraham, Isaac, Jacob, and Joseph), but this never leads to the idea that fortune and suffering, blessing and cross are mutually exclusive opposites – nor does it in the New Testament. Indeed, the only difference between the Old and New Testaments in this respect is that in the

Old the blessing includes the cross, and in the New the cross includes the blessing.

To turn to a different point: not only action, but also suffering is a way to freedom. In suffering, the deliverance consists in our being allowed to put the matter out of our own hands into God's hands. In this sense death is the crowning of human freedom. Whether the human deed is a matter of faith or not depends on whether we understand our suffering as an extension of our action and a completion of freedom. I think that is very important and very comforting. . .

Miscellaneous Thoughts

Giordano Bruno: 'There can be something frightening about the sight of a friend; no enemy can be so terrifying as he' – Can you understand that? I'm trying hard, but I can't really understand it. Does 'terrifying' refer to the inherent danger of betrayal, inseparable from close intimacy (Judas?)?
Spinoza: Emotions are not expelled by reason, but only by stronger emotions.

It is the nature, and the advantage, of strong people that they can raise the crucial questions and form a clear opinion about them. The weak always have to decide between alternatives that are not their own.

We are so constituted that we find perfection boring. Whether that has always been so I don't know. But I can't otherwise explain why I care so little for Raphael or for Dante's *Paradiso*. Nor am I charmed by everlasting ice or everlasting blue sky. I should seek the 'perfect' in the human, the living, and the earthly, and therefore not in the Apolline, the Dionysian, or the Faustian. In fact, I'm all for the moderate, temperate climate.

The beyond is not what is infinitely remote, but what is nearest at hand.

Absolute seriousness is never without a dash of humour.

The essence of chastity is not the suppression of lust, but the total orientation of one's life towards a goal. Without such a goal, chastity is bound to become ridiculous. Chastity is the presupposition for clear and considered thinking.

Death is the supreme festival on the road to freedom.

Please excuse these rather pretentious *'pensées'*. They are fragments of conversations that have never taken place, and to that extent they belong to you. One who is forced, as I am, to live entirely in his thoughts, has the silliest things come into his mind – i.e. writing down his odd thoughts!

To Eberhard Bethge   3 August [1944]

... I'm enclosing the outline of a book that I've planned. I don't know whether you can get anything from it, but I think you more or less understand what I'm driving at. I hope I shall be given the peace and strength to finish it. The church must come out of its stagnation. We must move out again into the open air of intellectual discussion with the world, and risk saying questionable things, if we are to get down to the serious problems of life. I feel obliged to tackle these questions as one who, although a 'modern' theologian, is still aware of the debt that he owes to liberal theology. There will not be many of the younger men in whom these two trends are combined. How very much I would need your help! But even if we are prevented from clarifying our minds by talking things over, we can still pray, and it is only in the spirit of prayer that any such work can be begun and carried through...

Outline for a Book

I should like to write a book of not more than 100 pages, divided into three chapters:

1. A Stocktaking of Christianity.
2. The Real Meaning of Christian Faith.
3. Conclusions.

Chapter 1 to deal with:

    (a) The coming of age of mankind (as already indicated). The

safeguarding of life against 'accidents' and 'blows of fate'; even if these cannot be eliminated, the danger can be reduced. Insurance (which, although it lives on 'accidents', seeks to mitigate their effects) as a western phenomenon. The aim: to be independent of nature. Nature was formerly overcome by the soul, with us by technical organization of all kinds. Our immediate *datum* is no longer nature, as formerly, but organization. But with this protection from nature's menace there arises a new one – through organization itself.

Now the spiritual strength is lacking. The question is: What protects us against the menace of organization? Man is again thrown back on himself. He has managed to deal with everything, only not with himself. He can insure against everything, only not against man. In the last resort it all depends on man.

(b) The religionlessness of the man who has come of age. 'God' as a working hypothesis, as a stop-gap for our embarrassments, has become superfluous (as already indicated).

(c) The Protestant church: Pietism as a last attempt to maintain Protestant Christianity as a religion; Lutheran orthodoxy, the attempt to rescue the church as an institution for salvation; the Confessing Church: the theology of revelation; a *dos moi pou sto* over against the world, involving a 'factual' interest in Christianity; art and science searching for their origin. Generally in the Confessing Church: standing up for the church's 'cause', but little personal faith in Christ. 'Jesus' is disappearing from sight. Sociologically: no effect on the masses – interest confined to the upper and lower middle classes. A heavy incubus of difficult traditional ideas. The decisive factor: the church on the defensive. No taking risks for others.

(d) Public morals – as shown by sexual morality.

Chapter 2.

(a) Worldliness and God.

(b) Who is God? Not in the first place a general belief in God, in his omnipotence, etc. That is not a genuine experience of God, but part of a prolongation of the world. Encounter with Jesus Christ. The experience that a reversal of all human life is given in the fact that 'Jesus is there only for others'. His 'being there for others' is the experience of transcendence. It is only this freedom from

himself, this 'being there for others', even to death, that is the source of his omnipotence, omniscience, and omnipresence. Faith is participation in this being of Jesus (incarnation, cross, and resurrection). Our relation to God is not a 'religious' relationship to a highest, most powerful, and best Being imaginable – that is not authentic transcendence – but our relation to God is a new life in 'being there for others', in participation in the being of Jesus. The transcendent is not infinite and unattainable tasks, but the neighbour who is within reach in any given situation. God in human form – not, as in oriental religions, in animal form, monstrous, chaotic, remote, and terrifying, nor in the conceptual forms of the absolute, metaphysical, infinite, etc., nor yet in the Greek divine-human form of 'man in himself', but 'the man for others', and therefore the Crucified. The man who lives out of the transcendent.

(c) Interpretation of biblical concepts on this basis. (Creation, fall, atonement, repentance, faith, the new life, the last things.)

(d) Cultus. (Details to follow later, in particular on cultus and 'religion'.)

(e) What do we really believe? I mean, believe in such a way that we stake our lives on it? The problem of the Apostles' Creed? 'What *must* I believe?' is the wrong question; antiquated controversies, especially between the different confessions; the Lutheran versus Reformed, and to some extent the Roman Catholic versus Protestant, are now unreal. They may at any time be revived with passion, but they no longer carry conviction. There is no proof of this, and we must simply risk starting from here. All that we can prove is that the faith of the Bible and Christianity does not stand or fall by these oppositions. Karl Barth and the Confessing Church have encouraged us to entrench ourselves persistently behind the 'faith of the church', and evade the honest question as to what we ourselves really believe. That is why the air is not quite fresh, even in the Confessing Church. To say that it is the church's business, not mine, may be a clerical evasion, and outsiders always regard it as such. It is much the same with the dialectical assertion that I do not control my own faith, and that therefore I cannot simply say what I believe. There may be a place for all these considerations, but they do not absolve us from the duty of being honest with ourselves. We cannot, like the Roman Catholics, simply identify ourselves with the church. (This, incidentally, explains the popular opinion about Roman Catholics' insincerity.) Well then, what do we really believe? Answer: see *(b)*, *(c)*, and *(d)*.

Chapter 3.

Conclusions:

The church is the church only when it exists for others. To make a start, it should give away all its property to those in need. The clergy must live solely on the free-will offerings of their congregations, or possibly engage in some worldly calling. The church must share in the secular problems of ordinary human social life, not dominating, but helping and serving. It must tell men of every calling what it means to live with Christ, to exist for others. In particular, our own church will have to take the field against the vices of *hybris*, power-worship, envy, and illusion, as the roots of all evil. It will have to speak of moderation, authenticity, trust, loyalty, constancy, patience, discipline, humility, contentment, and modesty. It must not under-estimate the importance of human example (which has its origin in the humanity of Jesus and is so important in Paul; it is not conceptuality, but example, that gives its word emphasis and power. (I hope to take up later this subject of 'example' and its place in the New Testament; it is something that we have almost lost.) Further: the question of revising the creeds (the Apostles' Creed); revision of the theology of controversy; reform of the training for the ministry and the pattern of clerical life.

All this is very crude and summary, but there are certain things that I'm anxious to say simply and clearly – things that we so often like to shirk. Whether I shall succeed is another matter, especially if I cannot discuss it with you. I hope it may be of some service for the church's future.

To Eberhard Bethge   10 August [1944]

... I can understand your no longer finding your memories 'nourishing'. But the strength of thankfulness continually gives strength to memories. It is in just such times that we should make an effort to remember in our prayers how much we have to be thankful for. Above all, we should never allow ourselves to be consumed by the present moment, but should foster that calmness that comes from great thoughts, and measure everything by them. The fact that most people can't do this is what makes it so difficult to bear with them. It is weakness rather than wickedness that perverts human dignity most deeply and drags it down, and it needs profound sympathy to put up with that. But all the time God still reigns.

I'm now working on the three chapters that I wrote about. It's as you say: 'knowing' is the most thrilling thing in the world, and that's why I'm finding the work so fascinating. I think of you a great deal in your 'solitude'...

To Eberhard Bethge   14 August [1944]

... There is hardly anything that can make one happier than to feel that one counts for something with other people. What matters here is not numbers, but intensity. In the long run, human relationships are the most important thing in life; the modern 'efficient' man can do nothing to change this, nor can the demigods and lunatics who know nothing about human relationships. God uses us in his dealings with others. Everything else is very close to *hybris*. Of course, one can cultivate human relationships all too consciously in an attempt to mean something to other people, as I've been realizing lately in the letters of Gabriele von Bülow-Humboldt; it may lead to an unrealistic cult of the human. I mean, in contrast to that, that people are more important than anything else in life. That certainly doesn't mean undervaluing the world of things and practical efficiency. But what is the finest book, or picture, or house, or estate, to me, compared to my wife, my parents, or my friend? One can, of course, speak like that only if one has really found people in one's life. For many today people are just a part of the world of things, because the experience of the human simply eludes them. We must be very glad that this experience has been amply bestowed on us in our lives...

[You] strive to live up to the highest demands. I've often noticed how much depends on what sort of demands we make on ourselves. Some people are spoilt by being satisfied with mediocrity, and so perhaps getting results more quickly; they have fewer hindrances to overcome. I've found it one of the most potent educative factors in our family that we had so many hindrances to overcome (in connection with relevance, clarity, naturalness, tact, simplicity, etc.) before we could express ourselves properly. I think you found it so with us at first. It often takes a long time to clear such hurdles, and one is apt to feel that one could have achieved success with greater ease and at less cost if these obstacles could have been avoided ... But one can never go back behind what one has worked out for oneself. That may be inconvenient for others and even for oneself sometimes, but those are the inconveniences of education...

For your new year I wish you – after you've returned to your family and into the ministry – a really great task and responsibility and at the same time the necessary calm to be able to write something very good from time to time. For myself, my wish is that our spiritual exchanges will continue to make it possible for our thoughts to arise, be expressed and clarified, and still more important, that in each other we shall always have someone in whom we can place unlimited trust. The readings for the 28th are splendid. When I think of you that morning, I shall keep to them. The question 'Is thy hand ...?' Num. 11.23 may perhaps remind us of some unfulfilled wishes and hopes. Over against this, II Cor. 1.20 says: God does not give us everything we want, but he does fulfil all his promises, i.e. he remains the Lord of the earth, he preserves his church, constantly renewing our faith and not laying on us more than we can bear, gladdening us with his nearness and help, hearing our prayers, and leading us along the best and straightest paths to himself. By his faithfulness in doing this, God creates through us praise for himself...

To Eberhard Bethge   [21 August 1944]

It's your birthday in a week's time. Once again I've taken up the readings and meditated on them. The key to everything is the 'in him'. All that we may rightly expect from God, and ask him for, is to be found in Jesus Christ. The God of Jesus Christ has nothing to do with what a God, as we imagine him, could do and ought to do. If we are to learn what God promises, and what he fulfils, we must keep reposing very long and very peacefully on the life, sayings,

142

deeds, sufferings, and death of Jesus. It is certain that we may always live close to God and in the light of his presence, and that such living is an entirely new life for us; that nothing is then impossible for us, because all things are possible with God; that no earthly power can touch us without his will, and that danger and distress can only drive us closer to him. It is certain that we can claim nothing for ourselves, and may yet pray for everything; it is certain that our joy is hidden in suffering, and our life in death; it is certain that in all this we are in a fellowship that sustains us. In Jesus God has said Yes and Amen to it all, and that Yes and Amen is the firm ground on which we stand.

In these turbulent times we repeatedly lose sight of what really makes life worth living. We think that, because this or that person is living, it makes sense for us to live too. But the truth is that if this earth was vouchsafed to bear the man Jesus Christ, if such a man as Jesus lived, then, and only then, has life a meaning for us. If Jesus had not lived, then our life would be meaningless, in spite of all the other people whom we know and honour and love. Perhaps we now sometimes forget the meaning and purpose of our profession. But isn't this the simplest way of putting it? The unbiblical idea of 'meaning' is indeed only a translation of what the Bible calls 'promise'.

I feel how inadequate these words are to express my wish, namely to give you steadfastness and joy and certainty in your loneliness. This lonely birthday need not be a lost day, if it helps to determine more clearly the convictions on which you will base your life in time to come. I've often found it a great help to think in the evening of all those who I know are praying for me, children as well as grown-ups. I think I owe it to the prayers of others, both known and unknown, that I have often been kept in safety.

Another point: we are often told in the New Testament to 'be strong' (I Cor.16.13; Eph.6.10; II Tim.2.1; I John 2.14). Isn't people's weakness (stupidity, lack of independence, forgetfulness, cowardice, vanity, corruptibility, temptability, etc.) a greater danger than evil? Christ not only makes people 'good'; he makes them strong, too. The sins of weakness are the really human sins, whereas the wilful sins are diabolical (and no doubt 'strong', too!). I must think about this again. Good-bye; keep well, and don't lose confidence. I hope we shall celebrate Renate's birthday together again...

143

Please don't ever get anxious or worried about me, but don't forget to pray for me – I'm sure you don't! I am so sure of God's guiding hand that I hope I shall always be kept in that certainty. You must never doubt that I'm travelling with gratitude and cheerfulness along the road where I'm being led. My past life is brim-full of God's goodness, and my sins are covered by the forgiving love of Christ crucified. I'm most thankful for the people I have come close to, and I only hope that they never have to grieve about me, but that they, too, will always be certain of, and thankful for, God's mercy and forgiveness. Forgive my writing this. Don't let it grieve or upset you for a moment, but let it make you happy. But I did want to say it for once, and I couldn't think of anyone else who I could be sure would read it with nothing but joy.

Did you get the poem on freedom? It was very unpolished, but it's a subject about which I feel deeply.

I'm now working at the chapter on 'A Stocktaking of Christianity'. Unfortunately my output of work has come to depend increasingly on smoking, but I'm lucky enough to have a good supply from the most varied sources, so that I'm getting on more or less. Sometimes I'm quite shocked at what I say, especially in the first part, which is mainly critical; and so I'm looking forward to getting to the more constructive part. But the whole thing has been so little discussed that it often sounds too clumsy. In any case, it can't be printed yet, and it will have to go through the 'purifier' later on. I find it hard to have to write everything by hand, and it seems hardly legible. (Amusingly enough, for productive work I always have to use German script, and then there are the corrections!) We shall see; perhaps I shall write out a fair copy.

Maria was here today, so fresh and at the same time steadfast and tranquil in a way I've rarely seen ... You ask how the smaller and the large work fit together. Perhaps one might say that the smaller work is a prelude to and in part an anticipation of the larger...

JONAH

In fear of death they cried aloud and, clinging fast
to wet ropes straining on the battered deck,

144

they gazed in stricken terror at the sea
that now, unchained in sudden fury, lashed the ship.

'O gods eternal, excellent, provoked to anger,
help us, or give us a sign, that we may know
who has offended you by secret sin,
by breach of oath, or heedless blasphemy, or murder.

who brings us to disaster by misdeed still hidden,
to make a paltry profit for his pride.'
Thus they besought. And Jonah said, 'Behold,
I sinned before the Lord of hosts. My life is forfeit.

Cast me away! My guilt must bear the wrath of God;
the righteous shall not perish with the sinner!'
They trembled. But with hands that knew no weakness
they cast the offender from their midst. The sea stood still.

To his mother   [Prinz-Albrecht-Strasse]
                                   28 December 1944

I'm so glad to have just got permission to write you a birthday
letter. I have to write in some haste, as the post is just going. All I
really want to do is to help to cheer you a little in these days that
you must be finding so bleak. Dear mother, I want you to know
that I am constantly thinking of you and father every day, and that
I thank God for all that you are to me and the whole family. I know
you've always lived for us and haven't lived a life of your own.
That is why you're the only one with whom I can share all that I'm
going through. It's a very great comfort to me that Maria is with
you. Thank you for all the love that has come to me in my cell from
you during the past year, and has made every day easier for me. I
think these hard years have brought us closer together than we
ever were before. My wish for you and father and Maria and for us
all is that the New Year may bring us at least an occasional glimmer
of light, and that we may once more have the joy of being together.
May God keep you both well.

    With most loving wishes, dear, dear mother, for a happy birth-
day.   Your grateful Dietrich

POWERS OF GOOD

With every power for good to stay and guide me,
comforted and inspired beyond all fear,
I'll live these days with you in thought beside me,
and pass, with you, into the coming year.

The old year still torments our hearts, unhastening;
the long days of our sorrow still endure;
Father, grant to the souls thou hast been chastening
that thou has promised, the healing and the cure.

Should it be ours to drain the cup of grieving
even to the dregs of pain, at thy command,
we will not falter, thankfully receiving
all that is given by thy loving hand.

But should it be thy will once more to release us
to life's enjoyment and its good sunshine,
that which we've learned from sorrow shall increase us,
and all our life be dedicate as thine.

Today, let candles shed their radiant greeting;
lo, on our darkness are they not thy light
leading us, haply, to our longed-for meeting? –
Thou canst illumine even our darkest night.

When now the silence deepens for our hearkening,
grant we may hear thy children's voices raise
from all the unseen world around us darkening
their universal paean, in thy praise.

While all the powers of good aid and attend us,
boldly we'll face the future, come what may.
At even and at morn God will befriend us,
and oh, most surely on each newborn day!

Index

147

148